GUNPOWDER JUSTICE

Julian Samora is professor of sociology and anthropology and director of the Mexican-American studies program at the University of Notre Dame. He is the author of *Los Mojados: The Wetback Story*, coauthor of *A History of the Mexican-American People*, and editor of *La Raza: Forgotten Americans*. Joe Bernal is a regional director of Action. He is a former Texas state senator who authored the first minimum wage law in that state. Albert Peña, a political activist who has held public office for many years, is now a municipal judge in San Antonio.

GUNPOWDER JUSTICE

★★

A Reassessment of the Texas Rangers

Julian Samora
Joe Bernal
Albert Peña

UNIVERSITY OF NOTRE DAME PRESS

NOTRE DAME ~ LONDON

Copyright © 1979 by
University of Notre Dame Press
Notre Dame, Indiana 46556

Library of Congress Cataloging in Publication Data

Samora, Julian, 1920–
  Gunpowder justice.

  Bibliography: p.
  1. Texas Rangers. 2. Police—Texas—Complaints
against. 3. Texas—Race relations. 4. Mexican
Americans—Texas—Social conditions. I. Bernal, Joe,
1927–   joint author. II. Peña, Albert, joint author.
III. Title.
F391.S22   363.2'09764   78–62969
ISBN 0-268-01001-3

Manufactured in the United States of America

Contents

Acknowledgments   vii

1 The Dauntless Spirit of the Great
  American Southwest   1

2 The Men in the White Hats   15

3 Los Diablos Tejanos   27

4 Shoot First and Investigate After   47

5 The Most Irresponsible Officers
  in the State   63

6 Get Your Man and Keep No Records   77

7 Los Cinco Candidatos   89

8 John Connally's Strikebreakers   131

9 A Relic of a Primitive Age in Texas   157

  Bibliography   169

  Index   175

Acknowledgments

We are indebted to a number of persons who in the final analysis made the publication of this book possible.

All of the material that addresses itself to the myths of the Rangers was researched by Dr. Américo Paredes of the University of Texas. We are indeed grateful to him for making this material available to us.

An earlier version of this book was edited by Ms. Ann Fears Crawford. She also researched much of the material pertaining to the activities of the Rangers during the farmworkers' strike in 1967.

Ms. Irene Hinojosa typed several versions of the manuscript in its stages of development.

Mr. David Samora researched the history of the Texas Rangers for this project. We used much of the information throughout the book.

We wish to thank Mr. Archibald Gilles and the John Hay Whitney Foundation for generous support, making this research possible. The opinions expressed in this report do not necessarily represent the views of Mr. Gilles or the Foundation.

In seeking a title for the book, we were tempted to call it *Los Rinches,* which is the term that most Mexican Americans use in referring to the Rangers. We felt, however, that although such a title would be applauded by many, it would appear to prejudice the analyses in the book. We are indebted to Dr. Ernesto Galarza for the title *Gunpowder Justice.*

J.S.
J.J.B.
A.P.

GUNPOWDER JUSTICE

The Dauntless Spirit of the Great American Southwest

The western peace officer is better known through fiction than fact. . . . Neither gone nor forgotten, he has been transformed, while the fiction of yesterday displays a tendency to alter the fact of today. (Prassel, 1972, p. 244)

WITH THE POSSIBLE EXCEPTION of the Royal Canadian Mounted Police, there is no constabulary in the world so famous as the Texas Rangers. Throughout their history, the portrayal of the Rangers in books, biographies, dime novels, comics, movies, and on television has made their name synonomous with law and order.

The image of the Texas Ranger stands as a symbol of the law of the West, the protector of civilized society. The "law" of the West, particularly as interpreted and enforced by the Texas Rangers, however, was designed by and for Anglos. It was based on the theory that the cowman and the farmer had an inherent right to the land but the Mexican and the Indian did not. In recent years, Ranger interpretation and enforcement of the law in Texas as it pertains to Texans of Mexican extraction, has been based not only on that theory, but also on the visceral belief that the Anglo has exclusive rights to the political, educational, and economic processes as well.

The role of the Texas Rangers in state law enforcement has gone through an evolutionary process since the establishment of "ranging" companies in 1823. Beginning as something of a paramilitary force against marauding and menacing Indians, the

1

"ranging men" soon proved to be effective in clearing the way for white settlers' expansion westward. They did not practice "discrimination" between warring and peaceful Indians; they simply pursued a course of ridding the territory of all of them. As we have often heard in the portrayal of the early West, to a Ranger "the only good Indian was a dead one."

The success of the Rangers in eradicating the major threats by Indian tribes was chronologically simultaneous with a new challenge to white expansion and control: Mexicans from the south did not want to give up the land that belonged to them. During the 1840s and '50s the Texas Rangers concentrated their efforts in the border areas on behalf of the new settlers, harassing the Mexican residents as they had the Indians. The Texas Revolution and the Mexican-American War provided justification for Ranger zeal in ridding the Texas territory of thousands of Mexicans and for terrorizing into submission those who survived. Once Texas earned statehood in 1845, all those "citizens"—now called Mexican Americans—residing within the new state boundaries were doomed to an existence of inequality, poverty, maltreatment by Ranger lawmen, and a judicial system that had no justice for the Mexican American. The "crime" of these people was simply that they had been born Mexican and lived north of the Rio Grande; for many the punishment was instant, often whimsical killing at the hands of the Texas Ranger.

The seeds of Mexican-American distrust, bitterness, and fear of the Texas Ranger lawmen were planted in the fertile region along the border between Texas and Mexico. Those seeds have been nourished by the Texas Rangers in their treatment of Mexican Americans for over 120 years. The Texas Ranger throughout those years has been eulogized, idolized and elevated to the status of one of the truly heroic figures in American history by Anglo literature and song. Due to a great deal of scholarly attention and media popularization, the Texas Ranger's image has enjoyed the reputation of unchallenged fact. The time has come to reexamine the history, role, and purpose of the Texas Ranger as a law enforcement officer; it is time to shed some light on the long, dark shadow behind the image.

The purposes of this study are to expose the popular image of the Texas Ranger to scholarly scrutiny and to analyze the reasons why the Texas Ranger has secured a tenaciously favorable reputation in the minds of the American public; to review Ranger history, its authority, and its relations with minorities in Texas; to document the cases in which the Texas Rangers have abused power and violated civil liberties; and, finally, to draw conclusions from the evidence presented.

The Texas Rangers—
How Their Story Is Told and the Image Created

In order to appreciate the special status and function of the Texas Ranger today it is important to understand that the cultural, social, economic and attitudinal factors of the nineteenth century that created the Texas Ranger have carried over into the twentieth century as muted threads in the fabric of Texas society. These threads have become most noticeably visible whenever the Rangers have been the subject of criticism or when Mexican Texans have organized in order to obtain equal rights under the law.

Texas history has been based in part on the reminiscences of "old-timers," whose anecdotes and retellings of the past have reinforced the Anglo view of the history of the West and the romantic notion that the cowman was always on the side of law and order. The Texas Ranger shared in the benefits of the glorification of the cowboy mainly because the costumes of the cowboy and the Ranger were similar and because in the storyteller's version a Ranger was, in a sense, the "cowboys' cowboy"—he was a lawman to boot.

One old-timer, Judge Orland L. Sims, has recounted the exploits of the Rangers with all the laudatory language that made the Rangers a legendary symbol of the "law of the West":

> I have known many lawmen who had to participate in gun fights and even kill in the line of duty. They were altogether a different class of men from their quarry. Among them were Rangers: Captain Jim Gillett, Captain Frank Hamer, Captain Bill McDonald, Allan Maddox, Bob Miller, Henry Glassock, Everett Townsend, Pete Crawford, Oscar Latta, and others, including officers in every service and of all ranks and grades. As a rule they were quiet, unassuming men, disinclined to talk of their exploits and never boastful. They all, without exception, had a deep aversion, contempt, and even hatred of law breakers of whatever grade. I only know of one swashbuckler, whom I will not name. Disliking violence, they never hesitated to use it in the line of duty, and they all got a big kick out of putting the criminal behind bars. (Sims, 1967, p. 25)

Judge Sims also portrays the Rangers as those strong, silent, courteous fighters for truth and justice:

> Of these lawmen, none have more of my respect and admiration than the Texas Rangers. They have none of the swaggering, swashbuckling attitudes attributed to them by many. They are quiet, courteous, efficient, and they are sure not afraid. Long may they wave. (Ibid., p. 32)

Old-timers and nineteenth-century writers are not the only ones who have perpetuated the image of the legendary Rangers. In her memoir of her native state, *I'll Take Texas,* published in 1958, Brownsville author Mary Lasswell waxed eloquent on the subject:

> When it comes to defending Texas, there is one body of representative Texans whose fame rings round the world: the Texas Rangers. Robert A. Crowder is chief of the corps, the first full-time chief of the celebrated organization in modern times. He is the personification of the universal image of the Texas Ranger. Lean, muscular, and laconic, Crowder wears steel-rimmed spectacles—a comforting touch, somehow— along with his conventional Ranger western attire. Fifty-five, a Ranger for nearly twenty years, Crowder is a man to tie to in

time of trouble. When he puts his booted foot up on a stump and starts to whittle, law and order has arrived. Chief Crowder, six Captains, and forty-five Rangers scattered across the state add up to a small force—numerically. But seeing any one of them at work is ample corroboration of the old saying: "One riot, one Ranger." One Ranger is all that's needed. (Lasswell, 1958, p. 315)

In 1973, on the occasion of the Sesquicentennial Anniversary and the groundbreaking for a Ranger Hall of Fame in Waco, Texas, President Richard M. Nixon issued the following statement:

For one and a half centuries the Texas Rangers have vividly portrayed the dauntless spirit of the great American Southwest, and relentlessly served the best interests of both their state and nation.

I welcome this opportunity to express on behalf of all Americans the deepest admiration for the proud tradition of public service that has earned you such a splendid reputation ever since our frontier days.

Your sensitivity to the needs of the times and your ability to respond to challenges remain, as then, an inspiration for all your fellow citizens. (*Dallas Morning News,* July 28, 1973)

Perhaps no one has lent more prestige and scholarly authority to the Ranger image than the renowned Texas historian, Walter Prescott Webb, professor of history at the University of Texas for thirty-five years and one-time president of the American Historical Association. The picture of the Texas Rangers as a fine, fearless breed of men, known for fairness and impartiality in enforcing the law, gallant on horseback, with Colt revolvers on their hips and steely blue eyes under their Stetson hats, ruthless in their treatment of the enemies of Texas, shy and gentle as lambs before white womenfolk, comes alive in the pages of Webb's *The Texas Rangers,* first published in 1935. (The 1965 edition carries a foreword by Lyndon Baines Johnson.)

The Webb account was so rich in imagery that it was promptly made into a movie, *The Texas Rangers,* by King Vidor Studios in 1936, and followed in 1940 by a Cecil B. DeMille production in which the Rangers join forces with the Canadian Mounties. Countless other movies, radio programs, and television series have relied on Webb's book as a source for authenticity.

Because of Webb's profound influence on the public impression of the Rangers and the reputation of his work *The Texas Rangers* as definitive history, it is incumbent on the authors to point out a few things to the reader.

That Webb manipulated his material somewhat in adhering to the popular image of the Rangers is a charge made by John Weaver in his book *The Brownsville Raid,* published in 1973. According to Weaver, Webb's original draft of *The Texas Rangers* included the opinion of Judge Harbert Davenport, a highly respected citizen of Brownsville who gained a statewide reputation as a historian, about Ranger Captain William McDonald: "I never found a Border man who had the slightest respect for Bill McDonald. He was, to them, a troublemaker, an advertiser, a teller of tales of which he was himself the hero, inclined to act—and act violently—on false or doubtful information, vain and self-important" (Weaver, 1973, p. 80). According to Weaver, this was pencilled out of Webb's final draft.

In the early 1970s, Dr. Webb was working on a revision of *The Texas Rangers.* Unfortunately he died before it was completed. His interest in revising his work, according to Llerana Friend in an article published in the *Southwestern Historical Review* in 1971, was to show that his attitude had changed toward Mexican Americans.

In the course of the research for this study, the authors have identified *The Texas Rangers* and other works by Webb on the subject as the chief sources in the perpetuation and institutionalization of Ranger mythology. Passages from Webb revealing his propensity for making personal characterizations which have passed as historical reality are included. It is the view of the authors that Webb's work has not delineated between myth and historical fact accurately enough to stand the test of time. Old-timers, new-timers, historians, moviemakers, comic book producers, newspapermen, radio and television producers have all told the story of the hero of the West. But none has been more prolific or successful in packaging and selling the image than the Rangers themselves. They have been their own most dedicated press agents: from the early frontier days through a century of stacks of autobiographies, climaxing in 1973 with the Texas Ranger Sesquicentennial Commemorative Celebration and the establishment of a Ranger Hall of Fame— the Homer Garrison Memorial Texas Ranger Museum.

One of the purposes of this study of the Texas Rangers, then, is to attempt to separate fact from fiction, the myth from the reality, and to update the history of the Texas Rangers in light of their activities during the 1960s and '70s.

The difficulties in distinguishing the myth from the reality in a history of the Texas Rangers stem from several problems. First, of the three cultural entities represented on the Texas frontier, Mexican, Indian, and Anglo, the Anglo written records are the ones that have survived. Second, the early polarization of the different cultural factions tended to confuse the issues and to bias the reports of anyone involved in conflict. Polarized factions tend to speak in hyperbole. Evidence of this is the creation of the term "Rinches" (for Texas Rangers) in the border area. The word seems to be roughly equivalent in emotional content to the word "pig" as applied to law enforcement officers today. The Rangers, for their part, thought of the Mexicans and Indians as treacherous and cruel, and considered them their hereditary enemies (Horgan, 1968, p. 703). Third, the Texas Rangers have become cultural heroes to the dominant society.

The Society behind the Image

To understand how the Texas Ranger has developed and flourished as the legendary, heroic symbol he has become, one must also understand the society which has produced this picturesque image. It is a society that wants the dauntless men to be heroes and the mustachioed men to be villains. The highly individualistic cowboy always wins; the "Injun" and the "Meskin" always lose. This Hollywood version of the Texas frontier, the home of the American cowboy, is, in a different way, not far from the attitudinal setting which produced the Texas Rangers and which continues to maintain them today. Many of the Old West and nineteenth-century social practices are quite obviously gone. But there persists in twentieth-century Texas a deep reluctance to let go of nineteenth-century attitudes.

The state legislature, for example, which screens, diagnoses, and passes judgment on value change, and which may be seen as a legitimate microcosm of Texas Anglo male society, is quite hesitant either to initiate or to foster social change. The latest expression of the legislature's reluctance to endorse political change was shown by its failure, while assembled as a constitutional convention, to submit a new constitution to the voters. After spending over \$3.2 million in a session lasting from January 8 to July 30, 1974, the convention adjourned (*San Antonio News,* July 31, 1974, p. 3A). Thus, the old constitution, a document which, Nimmo and Oden state, "represents a change less in regime values and goals than a fight over which interests were to be followed" (1971, p. 35), remains in effect. This constitution, adopted in 1876, according to McClesky, "was tailored to an age that is clearly behind us. The convention delegates made repeated references to the scalping knife and the Indian raids—spent considerable time worrying about policies to push the railroads . . . equally indicative was the debate on whether or not to have public education . . . that the state was too poor for the luxury of education. . . ." (1972, p. 25).

Although democratically elected, the legislature, composed of 181 members (31 senators, 150 members of the House
of Representatives), fails to represent the adult population. In
1971 there were only two black members in the House and one
in the Senate. There were ten Mexican Americans in the House
and one in the Senate. Women were even more under-
represented—one woman in the House and one in the Senate.
By 1974 there was some improvement. Although there were no
blacks in the Senate, there were two Mexican Americans and
one woman. In the House, there were eight blacks, ten Mexican
Americans, and six women, three of whom were black. This
was still far from a cultural cross section of a state with a large
population of blacks and Mexican Americans: major sections of
the population were far from proportionately represented.

In the main, the legislators "belong to the major Protestant
denominations . . . further distinguished by the thinness of
their ranks of the very young and the very old . . . higher,
socio-economic status . . . relatively high levels of formal
education . . . and with affiliation to the Democratic party"
(ibid., pp. 126–127). The party affiliation has been traditionally on the conservative side. In *Shadow on the Alamo,* a
dramatic exposé of corruption in Texas politics, Harvey Katz
states that Texas is "nearing its tenth decade of rule under the
Conservative Democrats" (1972, p. 4). Another trademark of
the Texas legislature is its position against organized labor.
"The conservative democratic faction has generally reflected
the interests of the upper middle class population, that is of
white, native born Texans, especially in white-collar or commercial occupation" (Nimmo and Oden, 1971, p. 64). Ironically, the blame for nonpassage of the proposed 1974 constitution was solidly placed on the back of labor. The fact that
conservatives insisted on including the "right to work" anti-
union principle in the constitution was hardly mentioned. This
anti-union principle has been a matter of statute in Texas since
1947.

The Texas Rangers, despite adverse publicity, numerous

investigations, and complaints both from citizens and from other law enforcement agencies, occupy a secure and almost sacrosanct position in the state. Their retirement pension is written into the present constitution (Article XVI, Section 66, Constitution of the State of Texas). The Rangers' position has been reinforced by their support of the dominant Anglo majority and by their help in maintaining the status quo throughout the state. In 1968 when the United States Commission on Civil Rights held hearings in San Antonio, one of the factors that came to the forefront was the predominance of the Anglo majority among the Rangers. The Commission's report states:

> As of October 1968, the Texas Department of Public Safety employed 1,640 uniformed and 109 plain clothes law enforcement officers, a total of 1,749. Of these only 28, or 1½ percent, were Mexican Americans. No Blacks were employed in the highway patrol . . . prior to the Commission Hearing there were 62 Texas Rangers, none of which was a Black or Mexican American. (1970, p. 15)

Guardians of the Economic Interests

From their earliest beginnings, the Rangers were closely allied with the economic interests of the state. One of their jobs was protecting the lives of Anglo settlers, it is true; but in safeguarding life on the Texas frontier, they had considerable help, notably from the United States cavalry.

The Rangers, however, had other important tasks entrusted to them—tasks which endeared them to the men of property along the Texas border areas. They safeguarded the Texans' property, like ordinary policemen, but their functions went much farther. The Rangers could and did ride into Mexico to bring back horses and cattle allegedly stolen from Texas ranchers. On occasion, they also rode into Mexico to capture and bring back escaped black slaves, who had made it to freedom on the "Little Underground Railroad" that went from central Texas through the Nueces Strip into Mexico. The Rangers, however, were more than protectors and retrievers of property in those frontier times. They also created the kind of conditions under which new property could be acquired by the Anglo Texans. By "vigorous action," as Walter Prescott Webb understates it, against nomad Indians and Mexican *rancheros,* the Rangers opened new economic vistas for their fellow citizens.

The only complaint from fellow Texans was that the Rangers did not work fast enough nor thoroughly enough. Ranger historian Webb comments that Texans wanted the Rangers to kill or drive out every Indian and Mexican in the state. "Texans demanded that the United States should muster the Rangers into federal service, pay them with federal money, and let them run all the Mexicans into the Rio Grande and all the Indians into the Red River" (Webb, 1965, p. 127).

The Rangers could be counted on to create a situation where the white man could become rich. The men who eventually profited from this "opening" of new frontiers were a select few, men such as Richard King and Mifflin Kenedy, who became great cattle barons in what once was the Nueces Strip. In turn, men like Richard King and organizations like the cattlemen's associations supported the Rangers with money and influence during the frontier days. It was to their advantage that the Ranger image should be enhanced as much as possible, to counter any criticisms that might be made about the Ranger force.

In the early period of their existence, then, the Texas Rangers served economic interests closely identified with Manifest Destiny. The Ranger was the guardian of an expanding frontier—an agent of expansion, in fact—and thus very much in tune with the times. His economic value to the entrepreneur made the Ranger a worthwhile subject for romantic image-making. Meanwhile, the Ranger could be as ruthless as he wanted in accomplishing his tasks. What was good for the great entrepreneurs was good for Texas. And, after all, the victims were mostly Indians and Mexicans.

In the second half of the twentieth century, however, the Rangers find themselves in a different situation. They still may be seen operating with all their old "vigor" in the cause of special economic interests; but such interests are no longer identified with the ends of patriotism, nor are their victims easily classified as "enemies of Texas." They often do have brown skins, but they are American citizens and taxpayers nevertheless. The victims of the Rangers' ruthless frontier tactics now are civil rights workers and members of striking unions.

The Rangers under Fire

The growing number of people who refute the image have been those closest to the Rangers—Texans of different walks of life and different ethnic origins, or those who have witnessed and followed Ranger behavior.

The history of the Texas Rangers, particularly in the twentieth century, is by no means devoid of criticism nor does that criticism come only from minorities. Citizen groups, state officials, and private individuals have called for investigations and at times for the abolishment of the force.

In 1919, state Representative J. T. Canales was moved to establish a series of legislative investigations based on very serious charges concerning Ranger activities. The documented charges involved murder; intimidation of citizens; threats against the lives of others; torture and brutality; flogging, horsewhipping, pistol whipping, and mistreatment of suspected persons; incompetency; and disregard for the law. The adjutant general was accused of refusing to investigate, covering up investigations, and keeping Rangers on the force after they had been found guilty of charges (the details are to be found in *Proceedings of the Joint Committee of the Senate and House in the Investigation of the Texas State Ranger Force*, 1919).

In 1925 John Elgin, a private citizen, challenged the constitutionality of the Ranger force, fearing it was becoming an unmanageable police force. The 1920s proved to be such a turbulent time, with the Texas Rangers creating so many incidents, that John Nance Garner, later vice-president of the United States, called for the abolishment of the force.

Dr. Américo Paredes of the University of Texas conducted a series of highly critical studies of the Rangers. The late Dr. George I. Sánchez, also of the University faculty, for a number of years commented on the unjust and unfair treatment of Mexican Americans by the Rangers.

In recent years Ranger activities have again come under fire. On May 13, 1967, the Mexican American Joint Conference passed a resolution seeking to abolish the Rangers. In 1968 Roy Evans, then secretary-treasurer of the Texas AFL–CIO, stated that the Ranger force had outlived its usefulness, was used only to break strikes, and was guilty of infringing on the civil rights of the citizens of the state (*San Antonio News,* January 10, 1968, p. 1). Also in 1968, state Senator Joe J. Bernal asked for, but never got, an investigation of the Rangers, alleging that they had failed to enforce the law in an impartial manner; and United States Senator Ralph Yarborough, a Texas Democrat, charged that the governor of the state, John B. Connally, had misused the Rangers, turning them into strike-breakers.

A United States district court for the Southern District of Texas ruled on a suit which was brought against the Rangers following the farmworkers' strike of 1966–67. The court ruled that the Rangers should be permanently enjoined and restrained from interfering with and discouraging peaceful organizing and from arresting persons without warrants of probable cause. On May 20, 1974, the Supreme Court of the United States upheld the district court's opinion on the charges brought against the Rangers. The events that led to the Supreme Court decision and the decision itself will be dealt with in detail. To understand the role of the Rangers in Texas law enforcement, one must study how their image and societal maintenance have given them license to perpetrate deeds that are beyond the law, and why it was necessary that they be stopped by the highest court in the land.

In considering charges of police brutality or malfeasance, people generally assume one of two things: the individual officers are "good guys," but the law enforcement system is outdated or corrupt; or, the system is all right, but some undesirables have made their way into it. On those rare occasions when Texans have been willing to admit that something might be wrong with their Rangers, the assumption has been that it is the individual Ranger who is at fault rather than the force itself; or, at most, that outside agencies have misdirected the efforts of the Rangers and all that is needed is to provide better direction. In 1859, and again in 1915, when armed rebellions by Texas Mexicans in south Texas brought bloody Ranger reprisals on innocent people, the excuse given was that "undesirable elements" had crept into the Ranger force. At other times, such as in the 1930s, criticism was answered not only by "cleaning up" the force of unwanted individuals, but by restructuring it or by changing the chain of command. Never has the response been an open willingness to question the continued existence of the Texas Rangers.

There have been other celebrated groups like the Texas Rangers in American history, but they were disbanded once their job was completed. Why the Texas Rangers became Texas's elite police force—instead of quietly fading away in the manner of Rogers' Rangers, Ethan Allen's Green Mountain Boys, or Quantrill's Raiders—is an interesting question, indeed.

The Men in the White Hats

THE MOST INTERESTING FACT about the Texas Rangers is that, though they function as a police force, they were not created as such, and did not operate as police during the early years when their traditions and operational patterns were being formed. In layman's terms, a police force is part of an organized community, working within and for that community. Its main function is to maintain internal order in the community. A policeman's duties may vary from pursuing and capturing criminals to giving first aid to accident victims and caring for lost children. He is supposed to be both a public servant and a functioning member of his community. In the final analysis, a police force is accountable to the people through the local electoral process. The Texas Ranger has never been accountable to the citizenry.

Ranger companies were not organized to police the communities of the colonists who had just declared their independence from Mexico. The Rangers were created with one main purpose in mind: to secure the rapidly expanding frontiers of the Republic, and later the borders of the state of Texas. Their reason for being was not to arrest drunks and chase bank robbers but to fight "Injuns" and "Meskins." In other words, the Rangers were created as a paramilitary force—as bodies of irregular cavalry. They were intended primarily as a "frontier pacification force." Their function was to repel Indian raids and to chase Mexican guerillas who raided into Texas retaliating for the cattle-rustling expeditions of Anglo-Texas "cowboys" into Mexican territory.

Indians, Mexicans, and Texans

Texas is divided roughly in half by the ninety-eighth meridian, which separates East Texas from West Texas, woodlands from forest. East Texas occupies the southwest corner of the Great Eastern Woodland; West Texas is the southern end of the Great Plains region. South Texas is in the Rio Grande valley; the boundary itself, of course, is the "great river," the Rio Grande.

In the eighteenth century the Spanish presence was felt in Texas primarily around the Rio Grande, although incursions were made farther north. In 1767 the Marquis de Rubí toured the Spanish missions in Texas and recommended to the King of Spain the abandonment of some of the Texas missions. Increased Indian hostility convinced the Spanish king to pull back the Spanish frontier in Texas from the southern Great Plains to the Rio Grande. Attempts to establish missions and presidios in the interior of Texas were abandoned, and a line of fifteen forts was established, stretching across Mexico from just below Laredo to the Gulf of California. All but two, Santa Fe and San Antonio, were south of the Rio Grande.

With the Spanish retreat, the southern Great Plains remained in the hands of the previous settlers, the Indians. The forest tribes of the East Texas Woodlands were primarily an agricultural people, living in permanent villages, while the West Texas Plains tribes were nomadic. The Comanche held sway in the eastern and central plains of Texas, and the Apache roamed farther west along the Pecos River and in the foothills of the Rockies. In 1824 the Cherokees settled in Texas along the Angelina, Neches, and Trinity rivers. "Other, though smaller, bands . . . came to or through Texas, running like frightened game before the devastating fire of the American frontier" (Webb, 1935, p. 7).

The coming of the Anglo to the Texas frontier in the 1820s completed a cultural triangle. This triangle was not allowed to rest until it more closely resembled a point, or a ray emanating from a single source. The triangle was composed of the Mexican frontiersman in the region along the Rio Grande; the American Indian, whose presence was most strongly felt in the Plains region to the north; and the Anglo, who migrated to Texas primarily from the eastern and southern United States. When Mexico gained her independence from Spain in 1821, Anglo colonization was subjected to the laws of the newly formed Mexican government.

The first attempts at colonization were begun by Moses Austin in 1820 and were continued after his death by his son Stephen F. Austin. After much negotiation, the first settlers in Austin's colony, located in the rich agricultural area around the Brazos and Colorado rivers, began arriving in 1821; and by 1824 the Baron de Bastrop had issued 272 titles to colonists (Richardson, 1943, p. 71).

The first mention of the word "ranger" occurs in 1823 in relation to Austin's colony. Stephen F. Austin "employed on his own account and at his own expense ten men to serve as Rangers" (Webb, 1965, p. 20). With the hostile Karankawas preying on the coastal shores of Texas, and with the Tonkawas raiding the Colorado settlements, Austin felt that protection from the Indians was important to the development of the colony. The "ranging men" that Austin specified were free-roving frontiersmen, armed and mounted on horseback, who would "range" over a certain area of the frontier to protect the colonists from Indian depredations. They were neither regular army recruits, nor were they members of a militia. They wore no uniforms, but ranged the area in the costume of the ordinary frontiersman. In 1826 a meeting of representatives of the six militia districts agreed to keep a permanent force of "twenty to thirty rangers in service all the time." It is not known whether this force ever took the field (Barker, 1925, pp. 165–166).

In 1825 the Mexican government, firmly established under the federal constitution of 1824, hurried the movement of Anglo Americans to Texas by promulgating a general colonization law designed to encourage foreign immigration. Immigrants were required to take an oath to observe the federal and state constitutions and the Catholic religion. New arrivals had to bring documents proving their "Christian and good moral character," and immigrants could settle in Texas through empresarios or on their own initiative (ibid., p. 137).

For five years, immigration to Texas flourished. Then, in 1830, the Mexican government, alarmed at the increasing American influence in Texas, determined to halt American immigration. The law of April 6, 1830, "forbade all foreigners whomsoever to cross the northern border without a passport from an agent of the Mexican government. It forbade all further immigration of Americans into Mexico, and it cancelled all empresario contracts" (Connor, 1971, p. 89). Reaction to the law in Texas was explosive. Disturbances resulted, which helped bring the colonists to contemplate revolting against Mexico. In 1834, (after the repeal of the law of April 6, 1830) American immigration into Mexican Texas was renewed.

Between 1830 and 1835 friction between the colonists and the Mexican government increased, with Anglo colonists outnumbering Mexicans by a ratio of six to one. Finally, on March 2, 1836, Texas declared her independence from Mexico.

The beginning of the Texas Revolution in 1835 marks an important point in the development of the unique role the Rangers played in Texas history. In October 1835 the temporary "Permanent Council," a revolutionary body, authorized the creation of three ranger detachments to range and guard the frontiers between the Colorado, Brazos, and Trinity rivers (Webb, 1965, pp. 22–23). The Consultation, a revolutionary body which succeeded the Permanent Council, added twenty more rangers to extend the protection of the frontier from the Colorado River to the Guadalupe. The Consultation provided for a military establishment consisting of a regular army, a militia, and a corps of rangers. On November 24, 1835, an ordinance was passed providing for a "corps of rangers" consisting of three companies of fifty-six men each. Each company was to be officered by a captain and two lieutenants. A major in command of the entire corps was responsible to the commander in chief (ibid., pp. 23–24). On November 28, three captains were elected, and R. M. Williamson was chosen to serve as major.

These "rangers," who served on the western frontier during the Texas Revolution, were distinct from both the regular army and the militia. They were not part of any regular armed force, and they had no flag or other equipment provided for the other troops. They were mounted on horses and armed, but they supplied both their own horses and their own guns.

From this rather inauspicious beginning the Texas Rangers rode into history. Walter Prescott Webb describes the conditions faced by the Rangers in their early years:

> By the opening of the Revolution the three races that were to struggle for supremacy were all present in Texas. The Indians held undisputed possession of the Plains; the Mexicans held the Southwest with their line of occupation resting on the Rio Grande; and the Anglo-Americans, henceforth called Texans, had virtual possession of the timbered portion of the then Mexican province. Since the three races were to wage constant war one with another, it was necessary for each to produce its representative fighting man. The Comanche had his warrior brave and the Mexican his *caballero, ranchero,* or *vaquero.* To meet these the Texans created the Ranger, who, since he was the latest comer, found it necessary to adapt his weapons, tactics, and strategy to the conditions imposed by his enemies. In spite of the fact that each of these fighters influenced the others, each remained the true representative of the customs and ideals of his respective race, a symbol of the fighting genius of his group. (Webb, 1935, p. 11)

Webb also assesses the enemies of Texas on an individual basis:

> Without disparagement it may be said that there is a cruel streak in the Mexican nature, or so the history of Texas would lead one to believe. This cruelty may be a heritage from the Spanish of the Inquisition; it may, and doubtless should, be

attributed partly to the Indian blood. . . . As a warrior he was, on the whole, inferior to the Comanche and wholly unequal to the Texan. The whine of the leaden slugs stirred in him an irresistable impulse to travel with rather than against the music. He won more victories over the Texans by parley than force of arms. For making promises—and for breaking them—he had no peer. (Ibid., p. 14)

Of the Indians, he states:

The wild Comanche and Apache were not amenable to the gentle philosophy of Christ nor were they tamed by the mysteries and elaborate ceremonials of the Church. The war-whoop was sweeter to them than evening vespers; the crescent bow was a better symbol of their desires than the Holy Cross; and it was far more joyful, in their eyes, to chase the shaggy buffalo on Pinto ponies than to practice the art of dry-farming under the direction of a black-robed priest. . . . War was the end and aim of the Indian's life. (Ibid., pp. 8–13)

Of the Texan, Webb has this to say:

The Texas Rangers represent the Texans in their conflict with Plains' warriors and the Mexican *vaqueros* and *caballeros* and in the fighting that followed they learned much from their enemies. In order to win, or even to survive, they combined the fighting qualities of three races. In the words of an observer a Texas Ranger could ride like a Mexican, trail like an Indian, shoot like a Tennessean, and fight like a devil. (Ibid., p. 15)

In his preface to *The Texas Rangers*, Webb gives us his opinion of the Texas Ranger:

When we see him at his daily task of maintaining law, restoring order, and promoting peace—even though his methods be vigorous—we see him in his proper setting, a man standing alone between a society and its enemies. . . . As strange as it may seem in some quarters, the Texas Ranger had been throughout the century a human being, and never a mere automaton animating a pair of swaggering boots, a big hat, and a six-shooter all moving across the prairies under a cloud of pistol smoke. . . . The real Ranger has been a very quiet, deliberate, gentle person who could gaze calmly into the eye of a murderer, divine his thoughts, and anticipate his action, a man who could ride straight up to death. (Ibid., p. xv)

People in the 1970s might consider Dr. Webb's characterizations of the Indian and the Mexican as offensive. However, his opinions are a decided improvement over the feelings of nineteenth-century Texans and their treatment of the Indian. After the Texas Revolution, the hero of the battle of San Jacinto, Sam Houston, became president of the Republic of Texas. Houston had lived among the Indians, and his policy toward the Indians was both a peaceful and enlightened one. When Houston submitted a bill to the Texas legislature that would have guaranteed the Cherokee tribe title to their Texas lands, angry lawmakers hastily rejected it. The Cherokee were a peaceful tribe; they had been pushed all the way from the mountains of Carolina and Tennessee and were now up against the Great Plains. However, "in Texans' minds they were merely marauding red men, standing in the way of rightful, Anglo-American progress" (Fehrenbach, 1968, p. 253).

The "Ranging Men" and the Republic of Texas

During Sam Houston's first term as president of the Republic of Texas (in keeping with his policies of economy for the new republic, and friendship towards the Indians) little is said of the Texas Rangers as an organized group. In December 1836 the Texas Congress passed a law providing for a battalion of "Mounted Riflemen" to protect the frontier. Five days later they passed a law specifying the pay of these "Mounted Riflemen" and making it clear that these men were "rangers" (Webb, 1935, pp. 29–30). This law stipulated that a battalion of 280 men be raised, each man to supply his own horse and arms. According to Dr. Webb, these men may properly be called

Rangers because of the reference to "the ranging service on the frontier" (ibid., p. 30).

In the following year, 1837, President Sam Houston was authorized to set up a corps of 600 "mounted gunmen" for "the better protection of the northern frontier" (ibid., p. 30). The men were to volunteer for a period of six months and were to provide their horses, guns, ammunition, and equipment. The corps was divided into three divisions with each division retaining a group of friendly Indians to act as spies. Although these volunteers were not spoken of as Rangers, it is quite obvious that they were intended for the Indian service.

On December 10, 1838, Mirabeau B. Lamar succeeded Sam Houston as president of the Republic of Texas. President Lamar's attitude toward the Indians was one of outright hostility; for him, the Indians were "merely trespassing vermin on Texas soil" (Fehrenbach, p. 255). He once said, "The white man and the red man cannot dwell in harmony together. Nature forbids it" (quoted in Webb, 1935, p. 27). This attitude, however, was not exclusively his. It was the prevailing attitude among nineteenth-century Texans.

Lamar advocated absolute expulsion and outright war against the Indians, and he instituted a series of campaigns against them. Under President Lamar, militia, Texas army forces, and local bands of "ranging companies" were used against both marauding and peaceful Indians. The expeditions against the Comanches were justified in Texans' eyes because of Indian raids on Anglo settlements. However, the wars against many tribes, such as the peaceful Cherokees, "were more in the nature of a land-grab" (Fehrenbach, 1968, p. 257).

During December 1838 and January 1839 several laws were passed providing for the protection of the frontier. The first law provided for eight companies of "mounted volunteers" for a term of six months. The second law called for one company of fifty-six "rangers" to protect the frontier in Gonzales County. The third law provided similar companies for Bastrop, Robertson, and Milam counties. The term of service for all these companies was six months. Another law provided two companies of "rangers" for San Patricio, Goliad, and Refugio counties. In December 1840 two laws were passed providing for "spy horses and spies" on the northern and western frontier.

The history of the rangers during this period is a rather confusing one. There is no continuous service to trace, and various laws authorizing frontier defense refer to "spies," "rangers," "mounted riflemen," "mounted gunmen," and "mounted volunteers." However, since all of these forces had certain conditions in common—not being in uniform, providing their own horses and guns, and serving for short terms—they are all accepted as part of the tradition referred to as the Texas Rangers. The job of these "rangers" was to serve in the frontier service, dealing with the "Indian problem." Although President Lamar would have preferred a regular army, the Republic of Texas did not have the funds for a regular military establishment. Thus, the practice of using ranging men for short periods of time, at less expense, became the norm for "protection" against Indians.

The Indians v. the Peace Officers

In January 1840, three Comanche chiefs rode into San Antonio to discuss a treaty. A meeting was arranged for March, at which time the Indians were to bring captured white women to the Texas peace commissioners. Neither side was completely honest with the other. Ranger Henry W. Karnes, the Texas negotiator, prepared to hold the Indians as hostages if they arrived at the conference without all their prisoners. On the appointed day sixty-five Indians arrived with one hostage. The rest, they explained, were still in the hills and were to be ransomed one at a time. The Texans prepared to take the Indians captive and in the fight that broke out several Rangers and most of the Comanches were killed.

Both sides were outraged at the other's violation of the truce. The Indians withdrew to mourn their dead and plan a raid into South Texas. In August 1,000 warriors rode to Victoria and captured two to three thousand head of cattle and continued to Linnville on the Gulf of Mexico. While the frightened citizens watched from boats in the bay, the Indians sacked the town and then set fire to it.

Captain Ben McCulloch and a company of Rangers intercepted the Indian vanguard in a small skirmish at Casa Blanca. The Indians were moving slowly enough to give Captain McCulloch, General Edward Burleson, and General Felix Huston time to muster 200 men and engage the Indians at Plum Creek on August 12. In a pitched battle, seventy to eighty Indians were killed; however, most of the Indians slipped around the Texans and headed west. Two hundred and seventy-five men under John H. Moore tracked the Indians to their camp on the upper Colorado and killed one hundred and thirty of them.

> The great raid on Linnville and the subsequent battles at Plum Creek and on the Colorado were the largest between Comanches and Texans in a half-century of hostility. . . . The Comanches continued hit-and-run raids on the frontier until 1876, but never again was there such a major engagement. (Connor, 1971, pp. 142–144)

In spite of successes in these early years, the Rangers had not developed a well-recognized tradition, nor were they a permanently established corps. In 1840, however, Ranger roots took hold as a result of the appointment of twenty-three-year-old John Coffee Hays as a captain of a "ranging company." Hays had distinguished himself as an intrepid leader in fighting against Mexicans from his post at San Antonio. It was during Hays' appointment, which he held until after the Mexican War, that Ranger involvement with Mexico grew. Between June 1841 and December 1842 Texas sent two expeditions into

Mexico and Mexico sent two into Texas. Twice the Mexican Army entered San Antonio, taking the city by surprise both times. President Lamar's policy of expansion and his dreams of a Republic of Texas that reached to the Pacific Ocean provoked the first invasion of San Antonio. Lamar sent an expedition to the upper Rio Grande to open trade with Santa Fe and to extend the Republic of Texas to New Mexico. The Texans marched some thirteen hundred miles through Indian territory and burning deserts only to be captured by the Mexican Army and marched in chains to a Mexican prison.

On March 5, 1842, Rafael Vasquez, commanding a troop of several hundred men, marched to San Antonio and in a guerrilla attack took the city, raised the Mexican flag, and declared Mexican law in force. Two days later the guerrilla force withdrew, with Captain Jack Hays's Rangers in pursuit. But Mexican President Santa Anna was relentless in his desire to retaliate against the Santa Fe expedition. In September 1842 a thousand Mexican troops under the command of General Adrian Woll again entered San Antonio and captured the city. Although the punitive expedition left San Antonio after several days, the Mexican forces took Texan prisoners. Loyal Texans rushed toward San Antonio, and Captain Hays's Rangers and volunteer troops skirmished with the Mexican troops before Woll's forces again withdrew across the Rio Grande.

Texans were in a mood to retaliate, and President Sam Houston, who had been elected to succeed Lamar, approved the organization of a force to invade Mexico. He also commended Hays and his men and approved their support of the expedition (Webb, 1935, p. 75). General Alexander Somerville's forces took Laredo; and part of the force, under the command of William S. Fisher, crossed the Rio Grande and attacked the Mexican Army at the town of Mier. The Texans ran short of supplies and were forced to surrender. Enroute to prison in Mexico, a few of the Texans escaped, but Mexicans forced the remaining prisoners to draw beans from a jar to determine who would be executed. Those who drew the black beans were shot by a firing squad, many who drew white beans later died in prison.

Despite his troubles with the Mexicans, Houston tried to make his second term a peaceful one. He determined to reverse Lamar's oppressive tactics with the Indians and began a policy of making peace treaties with the western Indians. Agents were dispatched to all the tribes with presents for the principal men, and Houston encouraged trading posts in Indian territory to supply the Indians with goods they had been getting from raiding Anglo settlements. Houston's agents met with the various tribes, held peace conferences, and began to make treaties of peace and friendship.

Although Houston disbanded the regular army, he was not able to dispense with the corps of Indian fighters. In January 1842 he approved a law providing for rangers for the southern frontier, and in July 1842 three companies of rangers were authorized: one company to range on the Trinity and Navasoto rivers, and two companies for the southwestern frontier. In January 1843 a company of mounted men was also approved for the southwestern frontier.

Houston learned the advisability of protecting his borders from the threat of Mexican invasion; and in January 1844 John Coffee Hays was authorized to raise a company of rangers to protect the frontier from Bexar to Refugio County. In December 1844 H. L. Kinney raised a company of rangers to protect Corpus Christi, and in February of the following year, both commands were extended. Kinney was to continue protecting Corpus Christi, while Hays was to expand his protection of the western and southwestern frontier. On December 29, 1845, Texas officially joined the Union, and the history of the Rangers during the period of the Texas Republic came to an end. Although the frontier "rangers" had seen extensive service against both Indians and Mexicans, it was not until the United States' war with Mexico that the Texas Rangers gained official recognition.

Los Diablos Tejanos

From 1840 to 1848, the period prior to and including the Mexican-American War, the Texas Rangers developed their unique spirit and acquired a reputation for bravery and service on the one hand and for ruthlessness and cruelty on the other, a reputation that is still with them. The Texas Ranger

> attracted the most bold and daring young men in Texas. Among these were John Coffee, "Jack" Hays, Ben McCulloch, Samuel H. Walker, W. A. "Big Foot" Wallace, Tom S. Lubbock, and George Thomas Howard, whose names have become commonplace synonyms for "hero" in Texas. (Connor, 1971, p. 135)

Of the Ranger captains, Webb states:

> To speak of courage among Texas Rangers is almost a superfluity. They all have it to a high degree, and the man who lacks it cannot long remain a private. The captain not only had courage, which may be a purely emotional thing, but he had what is better, a complete absence of fear. For him fear and courage are unknown; he is not conscious of either. This means that he is free, with every faculty about him, to act in complete accord with his intelligence. (Webb, 1935, p. 79)

The Mexican-American War

At the beginning of the Mexican-American War in 1846, General Zachery Taylor, in charge of United States troops in Mexico, asked Texas Governor J. Pinckney Henderson for four regiments. Texas responded with three regiments, of which two were mounted. The two mounted regiments, comprising about a thousand men, were commanded by Colonel Jack Hays and Colonel George T. Wood.

Colonel Jack Hays's regiment of Texas Rangers became a leading force in General Taylor's and later in General Winfield Scott's armies. General Taylor used two companies of Rangers to keep his lines of communication open. Being more familiar with the terrain, they were better suited for this job than the regular cavalry, who considered it a difficult and oppressive service.

During the war the legend of the Texas Rangers was first carried beyond the boundaries of Texas. According to Webb, the Rangers distinguished themselves as fearless spies and hard-riding fighting men. They became much-feared among the Mexicans. While camped at Reynosa for several days the Rangers began to build a reputation as "troublemakers" (Webb, 1935, p. 98). In the words of one of the Rangers,

> "Our orders were most strict not to molest any unarmed Mexican, and if some of the most notorious of these villains [i.e., Mexicans] were found shot, or hung up the chaparral, . . .the government was charitably bound to suppose, that during a fit of remorse and desperation, tortured by conscience for the many evil deeds they had committed, they had recklessly laid violent hands upon their own lives! *Quien sabe*?" (Reid, 1848, p. 53)

General Taylor, while appreciative of the Texans' fighting ability, realistically appraised them: "I fear they are a lawless set" (Webb, 1935, p. 99). Taylor further wrote that "the mounted men from Texas had scarcely made an expedition without unwarrantably killing a Mexican" (ibid., p. 113) and wanted no more Texas Rangers sent to his column. Of one of the few occasions that the Texas Rangers brought in some prisoners, J. J. Oswandel wrote, "This is one of the seven wonders . . . for they generally shoot them on the spot where captured" (Oswandel, 1885, p. 398).

Various incidents from the Mexican-American War show how the Texas Rangers earned the name among the Mexicans of *los Tejanos sangrientos*, the bloody Texans.

> One of the minor tragedies in this . . . war took place at the hacienda of San Francisco de los Patos in southern Coahuila.
>
> A unit of Texas Rangers acting as escort for twenty supply wagons rode through Patos late one afternoon and encamped about half a mile beyond the hacienda buildings. One of the Rangers remained behind to slake his thirst at the local *cantina*. Later, violently intoxicated, he staggered into the church, ripped down a large wooden crucifix, and proceeded to gallop wildly around the plaza outside, dragging the sacred symbol behind his horse. The inhabitants witnessing this act of desecration were rooted to the spot in their astonishment; their astonishment turned to horror and rage when the elderly priest tried to retrieve the crucifix and the drunken Ranger brutally rode him down. Blind with hatred, the citizens dragged the offender from his horse, tied him against a wooden cross erected in the plaza, and proceeded to flay him alive.
>
> In the confusion the Ranger's horse escaped and made its way to the American camp. Sensing trouble, the other Rangers immediately mounted and rode back to the hacienda and, as dusk was falling, they galloped into the plaza. They were greeted by the sight of their comrade, surrounded by a frenzied mob, shrieking in his final agony. With a yell of fury, the Rangers charged into the crowd, killing indiscriminantly. After clearing the plaza, they were forced to shoot their companion in order to end his suffering. Having wreaked their vengeance, the Rangers returned to camp. The Mexicans who had survived the carnage gradually emerged from the brush where they had taken refuge and began to gather their dead for burial. Don Jacobo Sanchez Navarro, owner of Patos, subsequently lodged a complaint with John Wool, commander of the army of occupation. The captain heading the Ranger detachment also gave Wool his version of the killings. It was finally decided by the parties concerned that, to avoid embarrassing the Army, the affair should be kept secret. (Harris, 1964, pp. 4–5)

Ranger John S. Ford noted in his memoirs:

> During the evening some rangers were about to enter a theatre. A Mexican sneak thief stole one of their handkerchiefs. The theft was detected. The thief was ordered to stop in Spanish; he ran faster. A six-shooter was levelled upon him and discharged. The Mexican dropped lifeless to the pavement. The ranger recovered his handkerchief and went his way as if nothing had happened. (Ford, 1963, p. 82)

Captain Parry W. Humphreys, an eyewitness to the incident, related this meeting between a Mexican and a Ranger:

> While the rangers were sitting on their horses a Mexican passed with a *cesto*—basket—of candies on his head. A ranger beckoned to him. He came near and the Texian [sic] took a handful of candy and ate it. He did so a second and a third time. The Mexican supposing he was being robbed, stooped down, got hold of a pebble, and threw it at the ranger with great force. The latter lowered his hand towards his holster—a pistol shot rang on the air—the Mexican fell dead. (Ibid., pp. 81–82)

Another incident, as related by Webb from Ford's memoirs, shows the arrogance of the Rangers while on Mexican soil:

> When Adam Allsens of Robert's company was murdered in a part of the city [Mexico City] called by the Texans "Cutthroat," the Rangers took a bloody vengeance. The Mexicans carried in their dead on a wooden litter. "At breakfast time they had brought in fifty-three corpses. . . . In the evening the captain reported more than eighty bodies lying in the morgue. . . . They had been shot in the streets and left lying." Complaint was made to General Scott. He called in Hays and questioned him. Hays boldly defended the Rangers, telling the General that no one could impose on them. Scott passed the matter over, but found work for the Rangers outside the capital. (Webb, 1935, pp. 120–121)

Ranger Ford makes it clear that Colonel Jack Hays, commander of the Rangers, knew what was happening; in fact, had heard the shooting, but did nothing to stop it (Ford, 1963, p. 84).

On February 2, 1848, the United States' war with Mexico ended with the Treaty of Guadalupe-Hidalgo, by virtue of which Mexico lost a large portion of its territory and the United States gained the land needed to complete its expansion to California. Mexico also accepted the Rio Grande as the boundary between Mexico and Texas, but the end of hostilities did not end the violence at the border. For many years to come, the Texas-Mexico border remained a place where quietness was the lapse between two outcries or two shots.

Texas in the Union

In the twenty-five years following 1848, the Texas Rangers fell into insignificance as a fighting force. With annexation and statehood in 1845, the United States assumed the responsibility of protecting the frontier, and the U.S. Army took charge of the Texas frontier. The Army built a line of forts in 1849 for the protection of the frontier; but settlement proceeded so rapidly that in the early 1850s a second line of forts was built further west.

The Texans, however, had very definite ideas as to how Indians should be treated. They grew very impatient

> with the clumsy methods and humanitarian policy of the United States Army. . . . The Texans demanded that the United States should muster the Rangers into federal service, pay them with federal money, and let them run all the Mexicans into the Rio Grande and all the Indians into the Red River. (Webb, 1935, p. 127)

The United States Army was dedicated to keeping the peace, and the Rangers were dedicated to eliminating the Indians from the frontier and to making the frontier safe for Anglo settlement.

The soldiers were circumscribed by many limitations that the Texans could not tolerate with patience. Soldiers could not kill Indians because of their mere presence. On the contrary, it was their duty to protect them. The Texans were wont to look upon [the Army] as game wardens and not warriors, and the Texans wanted an open season on all Indians. (Ibid., p. 128)

During the period from 1848 to 1858 there were intermittent hostilities between the Texans on one hand, and the Indians and Mexicans on the other hand. Ranger service for this period was also intermittent, and John S. Ford was frequently the man authorized to command detachments of Texas Rangers. The Rangers, however, never remained long in service, usually for a period of from three to six months; and the occasional nature of the work discouraged competent leaders and able privates.

The federal government and the state of Texas finally worked together to bring about a solution to the Indian problem in Texas. In 1853 Secretary of War Jefferson Davis wrote the Texas governor that if Texas would set aside lands for an Indian reservation, the government would see that the Indians were restricted to their reservations. In 1854 the Texas legislature set aside 70,000 acres, and the lands were established in two separate reservations. Semi-agricultural tribes, such as the Anadarkas and the Wacos, were established on the Brazos Reservation, and the Penateka Comanches were located on the Clear Fork of the Brazos. This attempt to quiet the frontier was, at best, ill-conceived; at worst, half-hearted. The amount of land set aside "was pitiably small; but the state insisted that caring for the red man was a federal problem and thought the grant quite generous" (Richardson, 1943, p. 203).

The Anglo farmers were hostile to the Indians, and the Indians, unused to an agricultural existence, refused to plant and tend their crops. No more than half of an estimated twelve hundred Comanches were ever on the reservation. Most Indians refused to enter the reservation; many of those who did enter soon left.

The years of 1858 and 1859 were bloody ones on the

frontier. In 1859 "in spite of the loyal aid the Indians of the Brazos Reservation had given the [federal] troops," (ibid., p. 204) the reservations were closed. The Indians of both reservations were transferred to the Indian territory north of the Red River in what is now Oklahoma.

> The move cost the Indians considerably. . . . When preparations were being made to leave, [their fifteen hundred] cattle were much scattered. Quite all of them were off the reservation. Captain [John Henry] Brown, commanding a company of State troops, said he had orders from the Governor of Texas to shoot any Indian he found off the reservation. He had the credit of refusing to allow Indians with passes to gather their own stock. In this way they were compelled to abandon nearly all their cows. They also left horses. (Ford, 1963, p. 454)

This must have been especially bitter for the Indians of the Brazos Reserve, many of whom had fought alongside of Ford's Rangers against the Comanches. After one engagement, Ford said of the Reserve Indians: "They behaved under fire in a gallant and soldier-like manner and I think they have fully vindicated their right to be recognized as Texas Rangers of the old stamp" (Webb, 1935, p. 158).

Except for a small band of Alabamas and Coushattas who lived on a reservation in East Texas, no Indian now had any legal right to be in the state of Texas (Steen, 1960, p. 218). However, the Indian problem was not ended. The "tame Indians" had been removed from the state, but the "wild Indians" continued their raiding parties.

The Cortinas War

After the United States' war with Mexico, Brownsville in the Rio Grande valley became a city controlled by the United States but predominantly inhabited by Mexicans. Political factions, machine politics, and election frauds were the order of the day, and the Mexicans were often the victims of injustice.

> The Mexicans suffered not only in their persons but in their property. The old landholding Mexican families found their titles in jeopardy and if they did not lose in the courts they lost to their American lawyers. The humble Mexicans doubted a government that would not protect their person and the higher classes distrusted one that would not safeguard their property. Here, indeed, was rich soil in which to plant the seed of revolution and race war. (Webb, 1935, p. 176)

Indignation ran high, and grievances piled one on another until a champion of the people arose to fight against Anglo oppression.

Juan Nepomuceno Cortinas lived on his mother's ranch northwest of Brownsville. Cortinas harbored resentment against the Anglos, shunning the life of a border aristocrat. He revelled in the existence of a *vaquero*, often venturing into cattle stealing, but always managing to escape conviction.

On the morning of July 13, 1859, Brownsville City Marshal Robert Shears arrested an inebriated Mexican with more than the usual brutality. Cortinas recognized the Mexican as a former servant of his and protested. One insult followed another until Cortinas drew his gun and shot the marshal in the shoulder, swept up his former servant behind him on his horse, and galloped away amid the cheers of his compadres.

Cortinas went into hiding, slipping back and forth into Mexico with the support of *vaqueros* on both sides of the Rio Grande. However, in the early morning hours of September 28 shots and shouts rang through the town of Brownsville. Cortinas had returned with a hundred or more supporters. The citizens of Brownsville remained behind doors while Cortinas's *vaqueros* flew the Mexican flag in jubilation over Fort Brown, opened the jail, freed the prisoners, and shot three Anglos and a Mexican. While Mexican Army officers crossed the border to liberate Brownsville, Cortinas rode in triumph to his mother's ranch and issued his rallying cry, "Our personal enemies shall not possess our lands until they have fattened it with their own gore" (ibid., p. 179). The oppressed Texas *vaqueros* flocked to join Cortinas's band while Mexicans rushed across the border to pledge their allegiance to the man whose name was already legend in Matamoros.

The citizens of Brownsville moved slowly against Cortinas, with the Brownsville "Tigers," under the command of W. B. Thompson, taking four days to move three miles out of the city in pursuit of Cortinas. When firing between the militia group and a band of Cortinas's *vaqueros* broke out, the "Tigers" charged for home, leaving their two cannons in Cortinas's possession.

Cortinas celebrated his victory over the Anglos by firing the cannons at six in the morning and by intercepting the mail, along with an Anglo to read it to him. However, he acted with great restraint, resealing the letters, hanging the mail bag from a tree, and sending the Brownsville citizens word where they could retrieve their letters. When his men captured cattle from a sheriff, he sent the owner word where he could find those the *vaqueros* did not use and enclosed a due bill for the eleven cows his men had eaten (Webb, 1935, p. 181).

Frantic appeals for help went out to the Texas governor and to the president of the United States. Captain W. G. Tobin of San Antonio rode with a band of Texas Rangers to aid the besieged town, and by all accounts the Rangers he brought with him were among the worst of the times:

> On the whole these men were a sorry lot, and their conduct for the remainder of the war reflects no credit on the organization. Harbert Davenport dryly remarks that Tobin had one good man, but unfortunately, he fell off a carriage and broke his neck soon after reaching the city. (Ibid.)

The Rangers broke into the jail and lynched one of Cortinas's followers, and in retaliation Cortinas marched against the Rangers, killing three men in an ambush. The two forces met at Santa Rita, and in the fracas the Rangers hastily beat a retreat back to Brownsville. Cortinas was proclaimed a hero, and more followers rushed to join his forces.

Cortinas once again eloquently appealed to the Mexicans to fight for their rights against their Anglo oppressors, but the main force of his followers came from across the border. The Mexican population of Texas failed to support the rebel leader. As United States Army forces moved toward the Rio Grande to support the Rangers, the governor of Texas enlisted the aid of John S. ("Rip") Ford to command all state forces on the border.

With eight men on horseback, few supplies, and even fewer guns, Ford set out. Gathering recruits enroute, Ford arrived in Brownsville in time to hear the fighting between the Rangers and Cortinas's followers at La Ebronal. Soon Cortinas was beating a retreat west of the Rio Grande, burning and looting as he fled, but always managing to keep ahead of the Rangers. When his army deserted him, Cortinas sought refuge in Mexico.

The Rangers fighting along the Rio Grande added to their record as troublemakers. Poor leadership and even poorer recruits led to the Rangers being feared by citizens as well as by outlaws.

> The state of Texas, especially during the 1850's, out of haphazard military policy and the usual bankruptcy, enlisted and dismissed a series of extremely dubious and damaging so-called Rangers in its service. The quality of these irregulars was entirely dependent upon the quality of their leadership, and of the captains of this era. . . . (Fehrenbach, 1968, p. 517).

J. H. Callahan's Rangers, pursuing a band of Apaches across the border, burned the town of Piedras Negras and rode back into Texas. Tobin's Rangers burned the fences and pens of one citizen for firewood and confiscated his animals and farm produce. The rancher wrote: "I estimate the value of the property taken by Cortinas at fully two hundred dollars, and the value of the property destroyed by Tobin's command at fully one thousand dollars" (Webb, 1935, p. 187).

In defiance of military regulations, but in the marauding tradition of the Texas Rangers, Ford crossed illegally into Mexico in pursuit of Cortinas, and the citizens of Mexico received the brunt of the Ranger raids. Mexican jacals were burned, Ford's men managed to engage the Mexican national guard in battle, and many innocent victims on both sides of the Rio Grande died. One estimate lists fifteen Americans, one hundred fifty Cortinistas, and eighty Texas Mexicans dead as a result of conflict along the border. Damages to property totaled in the thousands. When Lieutenant Colonel Robert E. Lee arrived on the border as head of the U.S. Army in Texas, he reported the damages to the ranches of South Texas: "Those spared by Cortinas have been burned by the Texans" (ibid., p. 192).

Although Cortinas's flight into Mexico ended the fighting in Texas and the Civil War drew many officers and men from the area, the legacy of the bloody Cortinas raids continued on the Texas-Mexico border. Cortinas continued his career in Mexico, becoming a brigadier general in the Mexican Army and governor of the state of Tamaulipas. However, the fame of the red-haired rebel lived on in Texas, with the citizens of South Texas living in dread of his return. As late as 1876, the *San Antonio Herald* reported that "Cortinas, the bandit, understands English, takes the papers, and keeps himself thoroughly posted about all important events in Texas" (*San Antonio Herald*, August 17, 1876, p. 1).

While Texas ranchers feared Cortinas, the Mexican *vaqueros* made him a popular folk hero, celebrating his exploits in the first *corridos* sung about a border hero. One stanza of an extant *corrido* refers to Cortinas's rescue of his former servant:

> That general Cortina
> Is very sovereign and free;
> His honor has increased
> Because he has saved a Mexican.
> (Quoted in Paredes, 1958, pp. 139–140)

The Civil War

By March 1860 the number of Texas Rangers had risen to one thousand. The Indian frontier did not warrant such a force, but this body of Rangers was part of a fantastic dream of Governor Sam Houston. There can be little doubt that he planned to lead a force of ten thousand Texas Rangers, with Indian and Mexican allies, into Mexico for the purpose of conquering Mexico and establishing a protectorate (Steen, 1960, pp. 243–244; Webb, 1935, pp. 197–216). However, the Civil War was too close to be averted and Houston's grandiose scheme was never implemented.

During the Civil War, the Texas Rangers were nearly nonexistent as almost every available fighting man was drawn into the larger conflict.

> Though many companies of Rangers were sent to the frontier, they were almost as frequently drawn off to the regular armies. . . .
>
> This all but total eclipse of the Ranger service is reflected in the scarcity of Ranger records in the adjutant general's papers in Austin. So much attention was given to the Confederate, and so little to the border service, that it is practically impossible to follow the activities of the so-called Texas Rangers. (Webb, 1935, p. 219)

From 1865 to 1874 there was no Texas Ranger service. After the Civil War the federal government did not allow the Southern states to keep organized bodies of armed men, and the problem of patrolling the frontiers was once again assumed by the Regular Army.

The Ranger in Song and Story

While Cortinas was being immortalized in border *corridos,* the Texas Rangers wrote their way into history. The period between the Mexican War and the Civil War saw the

Ranger legend celebrated in newspaper stories, dime novels, poems, and folk songs.

One of the first successful press agents for the Rangers was Captain John S. Ford. Ford also was editor of several Texas newspapers, and he used his newspapers to promulgate the Ranger image. He wrote about his own exploits and those of other Rangers in such newspapers as the *Southwestern American*, the *Texas Democrat*, the *Texas Mute Ranger*, and the *Texas Times*. A much-repeated statement characterizing the Rangers, one that has become almost a *sine qua non* in any eulogy of the force, can be traced to a piece done by Ford in the *Texas Democrat* for September 9, 1846: "A Texas Ranger can ride like a Mexican, trail like an Indian, shoot like a Tennessean, and fight like a devil."

Rangers and ex-Rangers were not particularly noted as writers of books unabashedly labeled as fiction, but they were great at memoirs and autobiographies. A cursory check of any Ranger bibliography substantiates the fact that Ranger memoirs and biographies tend to outnumber novels about the Rangers. Walter Prescott Webb has stated that the Texas Rangers are "masters of brevity when they speak of themselves—as economical of words as of pistol smoke" (Webb, 1935, p. x). However, Ranger reminiscences in print show that the Rangers have not been "economical of words" in publicizing themselves. And taking into account the tendency of the real-life Ranger to stretch the truth when it was necessary to make a good impression, one may wonder whether the Ranger biographies and memoirs should not be classed as fiction also. (For specific examples of Ranger exaggeration of fact, see Américo Paredes, *With His Pistol in His Hand*, 1958, pp. 25–26).

In the popular novel, the Ranger image was developed at a very early date. Scarcely was the war with Mexico over when Joseph Holt Ingraham published *The Texas Ranger* (1847). A decade later the infamous Mustang Gray was immortalized in a novel by Jeremiah Clemens (*Mustang Gray*, 1858). Like the histories, the stream of Ranger novels seems unending. Note, for example, *Captains' Rangers* by Elmer Kelton (1968), a novel about Ranger operations against border Mexicans in the 1870s; and *Rangers of Texas* by Roger N. Conger and others (1969), still another Ranger history—bringing the Ranger in print right down to our times. *Rangers of Texas*, by the way, includes a foreword written by Colonel Wilson E. Speir, director of the Texas Department of Public Safety, and overall boss of the Texas Rangers.

Beginning with the frontier years, Ranger image-makers have reached the average American at an early age, when vivid and long-lasting impressions are formed. Before movies and television, the dime novel performed analogous functions. Prentiss Ingraham's dime novel creations, such as *Revolver Billy, the Boy Ranger of Texas* (1883), and *Texas Charlie, the Boy Ranger* (1883), did yeoman work in establishing the proper attitudes in the young. Comic strips such as "Laredo Crockett" have taken over some of the functions of the dime novel in our day. Ranger image-makers also expressed themselves in verse form, often printing their compositions in local newspapers. Much of this newspaper verse was set to tunes taken from folk or popular songs, and some of the Ranger songs found their way into oral tradition.

Folklorists like John A. Lomax furthered the Ranger image-making process when they included such songs in their folksong collections. In his *Cowboy Songs and Other Frontier Ballads* (1910), Lomax printed both the ubiquitous "Mustang Gray" and "The Texas Ranger." Half a century later, the Pennsylvania folklorist Kenneth Goldstein collected "The Texas Rangers" from a fifty-nine-year-old woman in rural Scotland, who claimed to have learned it from her mother (1964, pp. 188–198). It is worth noting that, along with movies and songs about the Texas Rangers, the usual Texas prejudices against Indians and Mexicans have also been exported to Europe.

Even the "folk" songs about the Texas Rangers seem to have been touched by Ranger image-making. Such songs were once thought to have been communally composed; more recently, a number of possible authors have been offered for such compositions as "Mustang Gray" and "The Texas Rangers." No less a person than Texas folklorist J. Frank Dobie has opined that both were composed by an ex-Ranger named James T. Lytle (Dobie, 1966, p. 122). Countless writers have stated that as fierce fighters the Texas Rangers have had no equal. It could also be said that as self-image builders they have had no equal either.

As described earlier, however, not all Texas citizens of past generations have idealized the Rangers. Traditionally, Texans of Mexican descent have seen them as a bloody, oppressive force made up of men who were far from fearless or fair. The view of the Rangers held by Mexican Americans differs markedly from the conventional image. In discussing folklore in Texas history, Américo Paredes has contrasted these two views of the Rangers.

> The group of men who were most responsible for putting the Texan's pseudo folklore into deeds were the Texas Rangers. They were part of the legend themselves, its apotheosis as it were. If all the books written about the Rangers were put on top of the other, the resulting pile would be almost as tall as some of the tales that they contain. The Rangers have been pictured as a fearless, almost superhuman breed of men, capable of incredible feats. It may take a company of militia to quell a riot, but one Ranger was said to be enough for one mob. Evildoers, especially Mexican ones, were said to quail at the mere mention of the name. To the Ranger is given the credit for ending lawlessness and disorder along the Rio Grande.
>
> The Ranger did make a name for himself along the Border. The word *rinche*, from "ranger," is an important one in Border folklore. It has been extended to cover not only the Rangers but any other Americans armed and mounted and looking for Mexicans to kill. . . .
>
> What the Border Mexican thought about the Ranger is best illustrated by means of sayings and anecdotes. Here are a few that are typical.

1. The Texas Ranger always carries a rusty old gun in his saddlebags. This is for use when he kills an unarmed Mexican. He drops the gun beside the body and then claims he killed the Mexican in self-defense and after a furious battle.

2. When he has to kill an armed Mexican, the Ranger tries to catch him asleep, or he shoots the Mexican in the back.

3. If it weren't for the American soldiers, the Rangers wouldn't dare come to the Border. The Ranger always runs and hides behind the soldier when real trouble starts.

4. Once an army detachment was chasing a raider, and they were led by a couple of Rangers. The Mexican went into the brush. The Ranger galloped up to the place, pointed it out, and then stepped back to let the soldiers go in first.

5. Two Rangers are out looking for a Mexican horse thief. They strike his trail, follow it for awhile, and then turn at right angles and ride until they meet a half-dozen Mexican laborers walking home from the fields. These they shoot with their deadly Colts. Then they go to the nearest town and send back a report to Austin: "In pursuit of horse thieves we encountered a band of Mexicans, and though outnumbered we succeeded in killing a dozen of them after a hard fight, without loss to ourselves. It is believed that others of the band escaped and are making for the Rio Grande." And as one can see, except for a few omissions and some slight exaggeration, the report is true in all its basic details. Austin is satisfied that all is well on the Border. The Rangers add to their reputation as a fearless, hard-fighting breed of men; and the real horse thief stays out of the surrounding territory for some time, for fear he may meet up with the Rangers suddenly on some lonely road one day, and they may mistake him for a laborer. (Paredes, 1958, pp. 23–25)

Such is the Mexican-American view; and one could argue that the recent tarnishing of the Ranger image has occurred because the Mexican-American side of the story has finally been brought to the attention of other Americans. Times are changing and so are attitudes. In 1958, when Paredes's book criticizing the Rangers was published, it was reviewed in the *Texas Observer,* the state's liberal weekly. The thing that impressed the reviewer most about the book was that it was written in good English, although the author was a Mexican (Thomas Sutherland, "Book on the Ballad of Gregorio Cortez," *The Texas Observer,* February 21, 1959, p. 8).

The Ranger as Universal Hero

The attraction to the Ranger that is carried through in the historical tradition from the time of the war with Mexico to the present day is not the Ranger of the border conflicts, the pillager of ranchers, the burner of Mexican jacals. It is the "super-lawman," the good guy who always wins, no matter what the odds. An obvious reason for the appeal of the Texas Ranger is that he is dressed in boots and Stetson hat, with a big Colt forty-five on his hip. He is intimately related with the greatest of national images toward which television and the movies make weekly obeisance—the Great American Cowboy. Consider the typical cowboy hero in film and fiction: he is selfless, most often sexless, a passionless righter of wrongs, the hero who brings law and order into chaos by the simple expedient of shooting the right number of people in the wrong. The Ranger is, or pretends to be, the movie cowboy in real life. This explains the great popularity of the Ranger image far away from the border of Texas, so that Scottish cotters in the twentieth century are found by folklore scholars merrily singing about the deeds of the Rangers on the Mexican border. For we all know that—from the streets of Rome to the barrios of Bolivia—little boys love to play "cowboys and Indians," whether in Italian, Quechua, or any other of a host of tongues.

The Ranger, then, partakes of the romantic aura surrounding the American cowboy. It may be worth asking why the cowboy himself—in real life an unromantic workingman—came to be romanticized. Why did the cowboy become *the* image in the North American mythos?

The cowboy was not the only romanticized figure involved in the westward push of the United States. There were also the riverboat man, the mountain man, the buffalo hunter, the man of the forest, the drover, the cavalryman, and many others. Almost any one of these lived and worked under more adventurous and colorful conditions than did the cowboy. Yet, the cowboy managed to eclipse them all, and to gather into his own image important parts of the other figures. (See Américo Paredes, "El Cowboy Norteamericano en el Folklore y la Literatura," *Folklore Americano* 4 [1963]: 227–240, for examples of the way that older American folklore such as songs, artistic boasts, and anecdotes have been adapted into "cowboy" folklore.)

It has often been said that the cowboy was an especially attractive figure because he was a man on horseback. There is some truth to this, but other frontier figures also were horsemen. Much more important in the cowboy image is the Colt revolver on his hip, a symbol of the exaggerated cult of manliness currently known as machismo—a phenomenon that is supposedly Latin American, but one that has been part of the North American character since the days of Daniel Boone. (See Américo Paredes, "The United States, Mexico, and *Machismo*," *Journal of the Folklore Institute* 8, no. 1 [1971]: 17–37, on machismo in the United States as evidenced in the image of the cowboy and in prominent Americans such as Teddy Roosevelt and Ernest Hemingway.)

There is still another point on which one can draw a close parallel between the cowboy and the Texas Ranger, and this is in the tendency toward autobiography. The cowboy as a romantic figure was publicized not so much by popular fiction, as by the cowboy autobiography, which flourished a generation or so before the cowboy novel. Like the Texas Ranger, the cowboy was good at publicizing himself. There was, however, a very practical reason for the cowboy autobiography and other materials romanticizing the cowboy—an economic reason. During the period between 1866 and 1890, the cowboy was a participant in a flourishing business enterprise, the "beef bonanza." (See, for example, General James S. Brisbin, *The Beef Bonanza; or, How to Get Rich on the Plains* [1881; reprint Norman: University of Oklahoma Press, 1959].) The building of the cowboy image was part of this commercial interest, which was kept alive in part by romanticized cowboy autobiographies. The autobiographies, in turn, helped make the cowboy supreme over his rivals for the role of American "superman." In the years following the Civil War the cowboy and the Texas Ranger were even more intricately linked in the Texas trail drives, those dust-filled, hard-driving days and nights that have been romanticized in novels, songs, movies, and television shows. Both cowboy and Ranger worked to protect the economic interests of the "cattle barons" of Texas and became in history the Texan's Texan.

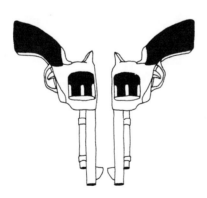

Shoot First
and Investigate After

THE LULL IN Ranger activities between the Civil War and Reconstruction years was followed by conditions that encouraged the legislature to reestablish the Texas Rangers into a strong force. The organization of a state police force under the "carpetbag" Governor E. J. Davis had proved to be both inefficient and oppressive.

> Civil affairs were in chaos as the result of five years of war and nine of flagrant mis-rule. The Indians, though weakened, still threatened and harried the western settlements, while bandit raids and cattle theft kept the Mexican border in constant turmoil. Inside the state cattle and horse thieves formed organized gangs while feudists carried on private wars and stage and train robbery flourished. (Webb, 1952, p. 755)

Feuds, cattle rustling, and raids by Cortinas's *vaquero* bands kept South Texas in a turbulent state. With the rise of immense ranches devoted to the raising of cattle and the resumption of cattle drives, Texans resorted to frontiersmen trained in the frontier tradition to deal with lawlessness centering around the South Texas triangle where the cattle industry was born.

In 1874 the newly elected Democratic governor, Richard Coke, and the state legislature of 1874 quickly reestablished the Texas Rangers. The Rangers were organized into two commands; a Frontier Battalion under Major John B. Jones and the special force under Captain Leander H. McNelly, who helped to reinforce the image of the Rangers throughout South Texas.

McNelly was a great captain. He was the epitome of the Texan in action, and he set a record of courage, cunning, and audacity that was never to be surpassed. McNelly himself was young, just thirty-one. He had been a partisan soldier for the Confederacy as a teenager in the Civil War, later served in Davis' State Police. Nothing was more revealing of his ability, honesty, and his reputation than the fact that he went from State Police to the Rangers with equivalent rank. (Fehrenbach, 1968, p. 575)

Captain McNelly and the Las Cuevas Affair

The Frontier Battalion was composed of six companies of seventy-five men sent to defend the western frontier. Captain McNelly was given one company of thirty Rangers and sent to South Texas to stop cattle theft and to return the South Texas counties to law and order. The Frontier Battalion was the more important of these two forces, but Captain McNelly's Rangers also brought attention to themselves, primarily in the Las Cuevas Affair, and in putting down feuds that had erupted in defiance of civil law.

Captain McNelly's reputation increased during the episode known as the Las Cuevas Affair. McNelly illegally crossed the Rio Grande into Mexico after a herd of 250 cattle and a party of Mexicans accused of cattle rustling. However, many times Mexicans were trying to retrieve their own cattle, lost or abandoned when they had to flee Texas in the wake of the Texas Revolution, the Civil War, or Anglo "appropriation." The captain had implemented a highly successful system of informers and sometimes learned the plans of the cattle rustlers in time to intercept their raiding activities. McNelly had received word of an expected crossing of stolen cattle at Las Cuevas and was determined to apprehend the raiders. He obtained a promise of a detachment of U.S. troops to come to his aid should he need it, and with that promise, crossed the Rio Grande to recover the cattle.

McNelly's spies had informed him that the cattle were on the way to the headquarters of General Juan Flores at Las Cuevas and that he could expect to find the headquarters protected by from 250 to 300 of Flores's men. McNelly's plan was to surprise Las Cuevas at dawn, barricade himself and his thirty Rangers inside a house, and wait until the U.S. troops came to his aid. "There can be little doubt that McNelly had some deep scheme in mind" (Webb, 1935, p. 256).

At dawn, the Texas Rangers attacked, under orders to "kill all but old men, women, and children" (ibid., p. 264). They surprised a group of Mexicans chopping wood for breakfast fires and killed them all. Unfortunately for the Mexicans, McNelly's spies had given him the wrong information. The Rangers had hit an unimportant rancho, called Las Cucharas. In his official report, Captain McNelly said (of the dead men) "they seemed to picket" (ibid., p. 265). Ranger Bill Callicott, who rode with McNelly's men, also described the scene:

> "We hit the trail the way we came. As we passed Cachattus Ranch [sic] there was nothing except the dead and they lay where they fell, on the woodpiles, and in the streets or roads. The women and children and old men were all gone." (Ibid., p. 265)

Realizing their mistake, the Rangers proceeded to Las Cuevas, ambushed the Mexican soldiers, and killed General Juan Flores in the fighting. McNelly sent for help and forty U.S. troopers crossed the river, thinking the Rangers were being massacred. McNelly tried to enlist them in an attack on Las Cuevas, but their captain refused. "Without doubt McNelly's cry for help exaggerated his distress, and was made for the purpose of bringing the federal troops into Mexico" (ibid., p. 267). The troopers were shortly ordered off Mexican soil.

In the ensuing parleys Captain McNelly refused to leave Mexico until the stolen cattle were delivered to him. The Mexicans agreed to deliver the cattle the next day at Rio Grande City, and McNelly withdrew to Texas.

Then, although the cattle had been promised, the Mexican officialdom resorted to further promises and delays.

Some cattle, not all the last-stolen herd but about half of it, were rounded up and driven to the river opposite Rio Grande City. Here, Mexican officials refused to see McNelly, and sent messages that they were too busy to move the cattle immediately to the American side. There was not only a real reluctance to return the property, but a determination to maintain Mexican dignity in the process, but this took forms that Texans found infuriating. . . . (Fehrenbach, 1968, p. 584)

McNelly sent a communication asking that the cattle be delivered at the "earliest hour," and his request was made more forceful by the presence of U.S. troops on the north side of the river. Seventy-six head of cattle were delivered to the south bank later that afternoon.

McNelly took ten volunteers and went armed over to the Mexican shore.

A Mexican official, backed by twenty-five heavily armed men, informed McNelly that the cattle could not be shipped across without inspection. McNelly, through Tom Sullivan, told the officer that the cattle had been stolen from Texas without inspection by him, and they could damn well be returned without it. The official was insulted, but McNelly was finished with Byzantine politics, parleys and devious duplicities. He ordered his ten men to form a line and ready their rifles. What happened next was told by one of the ten: The Captain then told Tom to tell the son of a bitch that if he didn't deliver the cattle across the river in less than five minutes we would kill all of them, and he would have done it, too, for he had his red feather raised. If ever you saw cattle put across the river in a hurry those Mexicans did it.

So ended another confrontation of Teutonic directness and Latin subtlety, leaving a sour taste on each side. (Ibid.)

The next day Captain McNelly had four of his men return thirty-five head of cattle belonging to Texas rancher and McNelly supporter Richard King.

In October 1962 Walter Prescott Webb published a story in *True West* magazine entitled "The Bandits of Las Cuevas." He received a letter from Enrique Mendiola of Alice, Texas, grandson of the owner of the rancho, Las Cucharas. Mendiola wanted "to set the record straight":

> Most historians have classified these men as cattle thieves, bandits, *et cetera*. This might be true of sóme of the crowd, but most of them, including General Juan Flores, were trying to recover their own cattle that had been taken away from them when they were driven out of their little ranches in south Texas. They were driven out by such men as Mifflin Kenedy, Richard King, [the] Armstrongs and others. (Friend, 1971, p. 321)

Part of Dr. Webb's reply to Mendiola, reads:

> I wish to thank you for your courteous letter about the Juan Flores Affair. I can understand that you, or any Mexican citizen or one of Mexican descent would be impatient with an account such as mine. . . . This account was written from Texas sources, report of Captain McNelly or of the U.S. Army officers. To get a balanced account, one would need the records from the south side of the river, and these are simply not available.
>
> There is no doubt that there has been some stealing back and forth across the Rio Grande ever since it was made an international border boundary. If the Kings and Kenedys and Armstrongs did not put their brand on other people's stock, they are about the only cow people of the age who failed to do so. These Texans even stole from one another. The unfortunate fact is that the Mexicans were not as good at keeping records as were the people on this side.
>
> You probably know I wrote the history of the *Texas Rangers* many years ago, went to Las Cuevas, and met the descendants of General Juan Flores who were still living in the village. I have often wished that the Mexicans, or someone who had their confidence, could have gone among them and got their stories of the raids and counter raids. I am sure that these stories would take on a different color and tone. (Ibid.)

Dr. Webb's reply to Mendiola was written at the time when he was working on a revision of *The Texas Rangers*. Unfortunately, he died before the revision was completed. He had wanted to bring the material up to date and to show certain changes in perspective and interpretation. Specifically, Friend notes, "Webb wanted to show that thirty years had brought a change in his attitude toward the Mexican-Americans because 'if a man can't grow in thirty years, he may as well be dead' " (ibid., p. 294). In reading Webb's last unpublished chapter, however, no change in perspective or interpretation can be noted. The accounts available from the Mexican/Chicano point of view are so different as to be unrecognizable from the original Ranger reports and Webb's interpretation. (See, for example, Paredes, 1958, pp. 15–32; Harris, 1964, pp. 4–5.) And, as we have already seen, one need not look exclusively in Chicano sources for reports that vary drastically from official accounts. (See Prassel, 1972, pp. 152–157.)

One of the Rangers who rode with Captain McNelly, William Callicott, recorded other instances of McNelly's forceful dealings with Mexicans:

> Casuse [Jesús Sandoval] would talk to the Mexican a little, and then tell Tom Sullivan, our interpreter, who was raised among the Mexicans at Brownsville, what the Mexican was. If the Mexican proved to be a citizen we let him go at once; and if he proved to be a bandit spy one of us would take charge of him and march along until we saw a suitable tree. The Captain would take Tom, the bandit, and four or five of the boys to the tree. Old Casuse would put the rope over the bandit's neck, throw it over a limb, pull him up and let him down on the ground until he would consent to tell all he knew. As far as we knew this treatment always brought out the truth.
>
> After the Captain had all the information he wanted he would let Casuse have charge of the spy. Casuse would make a regular hangman's knot and place the hangman's loop over the bandit's head, throw the end of the rope over the limb, make the bandit get on Casuse's old paint horse, and stand up in the saddle.

Casuse would then make the loose end of the rope fast, get behind his horse, hit him a hard lick and the horse would jump from under the spy, breaking his neck instantly. Captain McNelly didn't like this kind of killing, but Casuse did. He said if we turned a spy loose he would spread the news among the bandits and we would never catch them. We caught several spies on that scout before we overhauled the bandits with the cattle, and Casuse dealt with all of them alike, showing no partiality— he always made them a present of six feet of rope. (Quoted in Webb, 1935, p. 243)

Captain McNelly, of course, never reported his means of extracting "confessions and information," but claimed that he turned captured spies over to a local sheriff. Although Dr. Webb notes that there is no evidence to support McNelly's statement, "McNelly cannot be condemned too severely if he did permit Jesús Sandoval to send the spies to eternity by way of his paint horse gallows. . . . Affairs on the border cannot be judged by standards that hold elsewhere" (ibid., p. 252).

The Frontier Battalion and the End of the Frontier

When the Texas Rangers were reestablished in 1874, the Frontier Battalion was given the job of ridding the frontier of Indian marauders. Under Major John B. Jones's command, the six companies of the Frontier Battalion kept the last Indian raiders in check. During the first year and a half of Jones's command, he reported twenty-one engagements with the Indians, and twenty Indians killed. During the following six months, no Indians were reported in the area guarded by the Frontier Battalion.

By 1875 the northwest frontier was secured. During 1876 and 1877, however, Apache raiders were still active west of San Antonio. Texas Rangers, the U.S. Army, and the Mexican Army joined forces against the raiders, and in October 1880, Mexican troops killed the great Mescalero Apache war chief,

Victorio. The last recorded instances of Texas Rangers fighting Indians occurred on January 29, 1881, when the Rangers ran off a small band of Apaches. The frontier of Texas had moved into the far western portion of the state, and during the 1880s the Frontier Battalion moved west with the frontier. Major Jones died in 1881, and the principal captains resigned from the Frontier Battalion. After that, the Battalion lived on for many years, but it was "a living anachronism" (Fehrenbach, 1968, p. 592).

With the threat of the Indians removed, and the Mexicans subdued, an important point occurred in the evolution of the Texas Rangers. The Rangers now turned inward; they became a kind of state police. In March 1877, Major Jones had seen the direction of the times; he had ordered his captains onto the "suppression of lawlessness and crime," and had generally turned away from the pursuit of Indians (ibid., p. 588). The Rangers now turned their energies to pursuing domestic out-laws like Sam Bass and to bringing law and order to chaotic and lawless counties. They undertook their job with characteristic Ranger thoroughness.

> Local politics, and the law itself, hampered Ranger work in cleaning up the country. When McNelly . . . brought in King Fisher and a half-dozen of his men . . . the courts set them free. Fisher and his men were certifiably guilty of murder, but not convictable under the technicalities of the law. The Rangers had no patience with this; and a great impetus was given an old Mexican practice, the *ley de fuga* [law of the fugitive]. Ranger records indicate a large number of men killed trying to escape, or resisting arrest. (Ibid., pp. 589–590)

During the days of the frontier, the Rangers had had a free hand in controlling crime, but in organized counties they found it difficult to cooperate with sheriffs and other local officers. The local officers, of course, frequently resented the Rangers because of the implication that they were not competent to handle the situation.

> The [Rangers] maintained a somewhat sanguinary reputation. They occasionally adopted the Mexican *ley de fuga* by killing "escaping" prisoners and seemingly enjoyed comparative immunity in such matters, from the courts. (Prassel, 1972, p. 156)

Because of their zealous protection of private property, many big ranchers hired former Rangers as brand inspectors and detectives.

The Rangers' vigorous methods and their policy of "shoot first and ask questions later," have been portrayed in colorful fashion in the media. Many times the reality of the situation might be highly colorful, but not at all flattering to the Ranger image. One typical incident demonstrates the "straight" shooting of the Rangers of the Frontier Battalion.

> On May 17, 1885, Sergeant B. D. Lindsay and six men from Company D. frontier battalion of rangers, while scouting near the Rio Grande for escaped Mexican convicts, saw two Mexicans riding along. . . . As the horses suited the description of those alleged to be in possession of the convicts, and under the impression that these two were the men he was after, Lindsay called to them to halt, and at once opened fire on them. The elder Mexican fell to the ground with his horse, but the younger, firing from behind the dead animal, shot Private Sieker through the heart, killing him instantly. B. C. Reilly was shot through both thighs and badly wounded. The Mexicans stood their ground until the arrival of men from the ranch of a deputy-sheriff named Prudencio Herrera, who . . . insisted that the two Mexicans were well known and highly respected citizens and refused to turn them over to the rangers. The citizens of Laredo . . . were indignant over the act of the rangers in shooting on Gonzalez, claiming that he was a well-known citizen of good repute, and alleging that the rangers would have killed them at the outset but for the fact that they defended themselves. The rangers, on the other hand, claimed that unless they would have proceeded as they did, should the Mexicans have been the criminals they were really after they, the rangers, would have been fired on first. (Pierce, 1917, pp. 110–111; quoted by Paredes, 1958, pp. 28–29)

It is difficult to imagine that seven of those "fearless,"
"courageous," and brave Texas Rangers, so often portrayed in
western movies and television programs should have been
terrified of two lone Mexicans.

The Frontier Battalion continued as an anachronism until
it was disbanded in 1900, nearly twenty years after the closing
of the frontier.

> The Rangers exercised general power as lawmen throughout
> all of Texas, yet overstepped even those bounds. On several
> occasions detachments entered Mexico illegally on a variety of
> missions. They also were known to torture and lynch captives.
> Such activities along with other indictments of misconduct
> resulted in several trials throughout the state. (Prassel, 1972, p.
> 156)

On May 26, 1900, the attorney general of Texas ruled that only
commissioned officers had the powers of a peace officer:
"Non-commissioned officers and privates of the frontier battalion . . . referred to . . . as 'Rangers' have no authority . . . to
execute criminal process or make arrests" (Webb, 1935, p.
453). Under the attorney general's ruling, the battalion was
reorganized on a temporary basis but reduced to twenty-four
men with all arrests to be made by a commissioned officer. This
temporary force functioned from June 1, 1900 to July 8, 1901,
when a new Ranger force (limited to four companies of twenty
men) was authorized. After the turn of the century, altered
conditions imposed changes on the Texas Rangers. During the
twentieth century the duties of the Rangers have involved
protecting private property, policing migratory laborers, quel-
ling civil disorders in oil boom towns, and dealing with labor
disputes.

One Killing: Two Versions

An incident in 1902 involving the Rangers led to a very
serious situation. According to Webb, Sergeant A. Y. Baker

and two other Rangers who were scouting pastures on the King Ranch, came across a Mexican branding a calf. Sergeant Baker shot the Mexican, who proved to be Ramon De La Cerda, whose family owned a ranch adjoining the King Ranch. Although an inquest ruled that Baker acted in self-defense, "the Mexicans and their sympathizers" found "evidence" that the body of "De La Cerda had been dragged and otherwise maltreated. Public sentiment was sharply divided between the Rangers and those who for personal or political motives opposed them" (Webb, 1935, p. 463). Webb continues:

> The killing of De La Cerda was taken up by the Red Club, and inflammatory speeches condemning the Rangers by name as official murderers were published in a small Mexican newspaper.
>
> The Rangers, stung by the abuse heaped upon them and by the threats made against their lives, dealt harshly with their enemies. Ranger Puckett whipped a Mexican with his quirt for stealing his trousers, and Ranger [Harry] Wallis slapped a customs inspector who was supporting the paper that had been abusing the Rangers. Word came to A. Y. Baker that Alfreda [*sic*] Cerda, younger brother of Ramon, was seeking an opportunity to avenge his brother's death. (Ibid., p. 464)

Later that summer Ranger W. E. Roebuck was killed in an ambush attempt on A. Y. Baker's life. "Alfred De La Cerda was released from jail on bond, and on October 3, he was killed on Elizabeth Street by A. Y. Baker against whom he had been making threats" (ibid.). A subsequent investigation found no grounds for censuring the Rangers, and a grand jury commended the Rangers for their services (ibid., pp. 464–465).

The following account by Paredes gives a slightly different version of the story:

> Then there is the story about Alfredo Cerda, killed on Brownsville's main street in 1902. The Cerdas were prosperous ranchers near Brownsville, but it was their misfortune to live next to one of the "cattle barons" who was not through

expanding yet. One day three Texas Rangers came down from Austin and "executed" the elder Cerda and one of his sons as cattle rustlers. The youngest son fled across the river, and thus the Cerda ranch was vacated. Five months later the remaining son, Alfredo Cerda, crossed over to Brownsville. He died the same day, shot down by a Ranger's gun.

Marcelo Garza, Sr., of Brownsville, is no teller of folktales. He is a respected businessman, one of Brownsville's most highly regarded citizens of Mexican descent. Mr. Garza claims to have been an eyewitness to the shooting of the youngest Cerda. In 1902, Mr. Garza says, he was a clerk at the Tomás Fernández store on Elizabeth Street. A Ranger whom Mr. Garza identifies as "Beker" shot Alfredo, Mr. Garza relates, as Cerda sat in the doorway of the Fernández store talking to Don Tomás, the owner. The Ranger used a rifle to kill Cerda, who was unarmed, "stalking him like a wild animal." After the shooting the Ranger ran into a nearby saloon, where other Rangers awaited him, and the group went out the back way and sought refuge with the federal troops in Fort Brown, to escape a mob of indignant citizens. (Paredes, 1958, pp. 29–30)

"I Will Break Before I Bend"

The smoldering fire of hostility among the Mexicans of South Texas gave rise to another border hero who made both history and legend as the subject of the most famous of the border folk songs, "El Corrido de Gregorio Cortez." The variants of the legend surrounding the killing of Sheriff W. T. Morris of Karnes County by Cortez are as many as the legends of the Texas Rangers.

Born on a Mexican ranch between Matamoros and Reynosa on June 22, 1875, Cortez moved with his family to Texas in 1887. Although his family lived in Manor, Gregorio followed his older brother to Karnes County to work as a *vaquero* and farmhand. Cortez had never been accused of a crime before the hot summer day on June 12, 1901, when

Sheriff Morris rode up to his house looking for a Mexican horse thief "with a big red broad-brimmed Mexican hat" (ibid., p. 59).

A deputy, who claimed to understand Spanish, acted as interpreter between Cortez and Morris while Morris questioned Cortez about a mare he had traded to Andrés Villarreal. Cortez answered "no" to the deputy's question. if he had traded a *caballo*. The Spanish word for "mare" is *yegua*, but with Cortez's negative answer, Morris told his deputy to inform the brothers he was going to arrest them. Then there ensued another misunderstanding involving the use of Spanish. Gregorio replied to the sheriff with a phrase using the Spanish words *arrestar* (to arrest) and *nada* (nothing). The deputy later testified that Cortez had said, "No white man can arrest me"; Cortez's lawyer argued that he said, "You can't arrest me for nothing." Whatever the words, Morris understood them to be, "No white man can arrest me." The sheriff drew his pistol and shot Cortez's brother, and when he turned back to Gregorio, he found him with a pistol in his hand. The sheriff fired at Gregorio, missing him; Cortez aimed and fired, hitting the sheriff. Morris fired at Cortez several more times, reeled toward the gate, and fell. Cortez then shot Morris again as he lay on the ground.

Then begins a saga that matches the legend. Within a few minutes, the Cortez family fled the house. Morris staggered from the yard, but fell dead before he could reach help. A posse from nearby Kenedy set out in pursuit of Cortez and his wounded brother. Cortez managed to get his brother to safety, and then walked eighty miles to seek refuge with a friend, Martín Robledo, at the Schnabel Ranch.

Sheriff Robert M. Glover and the posse in search of Cortez ambushed him at the Robledo house in a battle described as "a tale of bravery unsurpassed on the part of the officers and of desperation on the part of the Mexicans" (*San Antonio Express*, June 16, 1901, p. 1). When the shooting was over,

Sheriff Glover lay dead, shot by Cortez, and another officer was killed by a deputy. However, the report the officers gave the newspapers told quite a different story:

> On the Robledo premises, the brave officers told the newspapers, they found an "arsenal" of ten Winchester rifles and "a lard bucket full of cartridges." A couple of days later the ten rifles had become eight. By the time of the Gonzales trial a month later, the ten rifles had become one Winchester rifle and one single-barreled shotgun, more in keeping with the normal country household of the time. The weapons had not been used the night of the shooting, Deputy Swift testified. It was evident by that time that except for Cortez's shooting on Glover all the firing had been done by the brave and fearless officers, who had merely followed a long-established custom, that of shooting first and looking afterward. (Paredes, 1958, p. 72)

Cortez headed for the border, saddling a little brown mare from a field, to help in his flight. Posses headed in pursuit, and "at least six horses were killed by one posse in pursuing Cortez and the little mare" (ibid., p. 74). Exhausted, the hunted man stopped to rest and then proceeded on foot as far as the little town of El Sauz, thirty miles from the Rio Grande. He bought new clothes, changed his money, and headed for Mexico. When Cortez stopped to rest at a sheep camp, Jesús González, known as "El Teco," spotted him and informed the Rangers, hoping to collect the thousand-dollar reward offered for Cortez's arrest.

Although Texas Ranger Captain J. H. Rogers later corrected the newspaper accounts of Cortez's arrest, the story that has come down in history is that of one Ranger capturing a desperado single-handedly. However, Cortez

> had been chased by hundreds of men, in parties up to three hundred. He had killed two sheriffs and fought off many posses. But for his capture all that was needed was one Texas Ranger, with the incidental assistance of another man, a former Ranger. Or so the papers said. (Ibid., p. 79)

Newspaper accounts of Cortez's capture did much to support the Ranger as hero legend, particularly since the Rangers were under fire from many quarters in the first quarter of the twentieth century. One interesting incident has to do with the reward offered for Cortez's capture. Ranger Captain Rogers refused any part of the reward money, suggesting that all the bounty be given to the informer González. However, González got only about two hundred dollars, with the rest of the money divided among members of the posse, "including a Karnes County deputy who took no part in the capture" (ibid., p. 83).

The indignation heaped on members of Cortez's family and friends did not cease with Cortez's imprisonment. During the posse's pursuit of Cortez, they had hanged one of the Robledo boys "until his tongue protruded and life was nearly extinct" (*San Antonio Express,* June 16, 1901, p. 1; quoted in Paredes, 1958, p. 71). When the boy refused to give information, members of the Robledo family were imprisoned in San Antonio. In addition, the members of Cortez's family were jailed. Although the children were released after Cortez's capture, the adults were kept in jail for four months without any charges being brought against them.

Cortez was tried in Corpus Christi for the murder of Sheriff Morris and the jury brought in a verdict of not guilty. When Cortez was tried in Columbus for killing Sheriff Glover, he was sentenced to life in prison. During the three-and-one-half-year legal battle, Cortez spent all the time in jail—"eleven jails in eleven counties of Texas" (Paredes, 1958, p. 94). The "famous Mexican" went to the state penitentiary at Huntsville, and after twelve years he was pardoned by Governor Oscar B. Colquitt.

Cortez's stand against the forces of law and order in Texas was soon celebrated in *cuento* and *corrido,* but the troubles between Anglos and Mexicans on the Texas border failed to subside with Cortez's capture and imprisonment. In fact, until the 1920s the area was torn with so much strife and turmoil that it earned the reputation as the "bloody border."

The Most Irresponsible
Officers in the State

THE STORY OF the Texas Rangers prior to and during World War I marks one of the worst episodes in Ranger history. "By 1900 the force was notoriously corrupt, and during World War I the Rangers became little more than terrorists, a racist army supported by the state for the purpose of intimidating Mexicans on both sides of the Border" (*Time* January 7, 1977, pp. 88–89).

Increasing dissatisfaction with the Rangers, especially in East Texas, led state Representative Cox of Ellis County to attempt to eliminate the Ranger force by striking their appropriation from the budget. Cox declared that

> there is more danger from the Rangers than from the men they are supposed to hunt down; . . . there is no authority of law for the Ranger force; . . . they are the most irresponsible officers in the State. (Quoted in Paredes, 1958, p. 31)

John Nance Garner, future vice-president of the United States, was also one who, early in the twentieth century, advocated the abolishing of the Rangers (ibid.).

Tension along the border was aggravated by Mexico's internal struggles. The turbulent conditions were primarily caused by the Mexican Revolution of 1910, and diplomatic relations between Mexico and the United States were often shaky. In 1911 Governor Oscar B. Colquitt had declared that Texas would remain neutral over revolutionary activities, that contraband could not be carried across the state, and that all

Mexican revolutionaries would have to leave Texas. However, border troubles continued with Mexican revolutionary Pancho Villa's fighting along the Texas border near El Paso becoming so intense that "American hostesses served tea to their guests on the flat roofs of their houses and supplied field glasses for them to survey the battles" (Crawford, 1971, p. 4).

Villa raided the lower Rio Grande valley during 1915, and Colquitt's successor, Governor James E. Ferguson, requested aid from President Woodrow Wilson. Major General Frederick Funston investigated raids along the border, but "remained convinced that the cause lay with Texans and not with Mexicans" (ibid., p. 13). In June 1915 Ferguson requested $30,000 from Congress to send thirty additional Texas Rangers to the border, and Funston agreed with Ferguson that "federal funds should be granted to the state for preserving law and order along the border" (ibid., p. 15).

Revolutionaries and counter-revolutionaries used the border region to assemble armies and to accumulate arms and ammunition, and in 1915 the discovery of the Plan de San Diego added to the confusion and tension. The Plan was "conceived by supporters of [Victoriano] Huerta and Pascual Orozco and financed by the German government in order to keep the United States occupied in Mexico and to prevent her interfering in the impending war in Europe" (ibid.). According to the Plan, an uprising of Mexican citizens and American citizens of Mexican descent would capture the Southwestern states, including Texas, and annex them to Mexico. Raiders under Aniceto Pizaña increased apprehension along the border by killing two Americans at San Benito and by robbing a train at Brownsville, killing one soldier and one civilian.

The Zimmerman Note, made public in March 1917, added to the hostile feelings of Texans toward citizens of Mexican descent. This note, from the German foreign secretary to the German ambassador in Mexico, proposed German support of a Mexican invasion of the United States for the purpose of Mexican annexation of Texas, New Mexico, and

Arizona. The Mexican government did not accept the proposal, but much suspicion was aroused because the United States learned of the note from the British Secret Service, not from Mexico.

> The situation can be summed up by saying that after the troubles developed the Americans instituted a reign of terror against the Mexicans and that many innocent Mexicans were made to suffer. . . . In the orgy of bloodshed that followed, the Texas Rangers played a prominent part, and one of which many members of the force have been heartily ashamed. (Webb, 1935, p. 478)

Webb notes that the number of people killed in the Rio Grande valley between 1915 and 1920 will never be known; the estimates range from 500 to 5,000. (In 1917 an entire company of Rangers was discharged following indiscriminate arrests.)

The confusion and tension of the times provoked a violent reaction against all Mexicans in the Rio Grande valley, and President Wilson placed large numbers of Army regulars and National Guardsmen in the valley. The Texas Rangers were expanded to approximately one thousand men; most of them in the border service.

In retaliation for crimes against Americans, Rangers and local posses lashed out against border Mexicans. In keeping with their tradition and history, the Rangers "shot first and investigated afterward" (Fehrenbach, 1968, p. 691).

> [The Texas Rangers] waged persecution. . . . There were numerous cases of flogging, torture, threatened castration, and legalized murder. Even some of this was justified by events, since the Rangers faced some of the cruelest outlaws who ever lived. But enough of this reprisal fell on people innocent of any crime but the one of being Mexican to discredit the whole.
> One incident testified to by Sheriff W. T. Vann of Cameron County was illustrative of some hundred others. On October 18, 1915, Mexican bandits wrecked and looted a passenger train six miles north of Brownsville. Sheriff Vann and a party of Rangers

captured four men suspected of having taken part in the attack. The Rangers decided to take the captives into the brush and shoot them, since they had had poor experience in getting convictions at trials. Vann refused to take part in this and was told by one Ranger: "If you do not have the guts to do it, I will." The four Mexicans were shot. (Ibid., p. 692)

These were serious times, but, as many local law enforcement officers testified later, the Rangers' actions were unjustified. The United States and Texas had 35,000 troops on the border in 1917. Texas was in no danger from Mexico. It must be said that the Rangers were not alone in this reprisal against people whose main crime was being born with brown skin or a Spanish name. Local citizens and sheriffs, and in some cases the Army, shared the Rangers' culpability.

Rather than allaying the tensions on the border, the Texas Rangers did much to inflame them. Ranger operations encouraged an abiding hostility for American authority and provoked violent fear and hatred among Spanish-speaking people. So deeply was this felt that "even third and fourth generation citizens, who had never actually seen a Ranger, reacted with an instinctive phobia toward the name" (ibid., p. 693).

In the twentieth century the Texas Rangers were an anachronism; and by 1919, at the end of an exhaustive legislative investigation, the Rangers were badly discredited.

The investigation was the work of J. T. Canales, a state representative from Brownsville, who had introduced a bill to reorganize and upgrade the Ranger force by raising their pay and their qualifications. He was accused of wanting to abolish the Texas Rangers, but he claimed that his aim was to remove the force from politics and to rid the force of unqualified and vicious men (ibid.). To this end he introduced some twenty well-documented charges of Ranger atrocities, ruthlessness, and irresponsibility, including alleged wanton killing, flogging, torture of prisoners, drunkenness, and assault. Among the charges was one in which the adjutant general was charged with using the Rangers for political purposes. "The burden of Mr.

Canales's complaints, however, was against the Rangers for the maltreatment of Mexicans" (Webb, 1935, p. 514). Webb points out:

> In answer to the question as to how the Mexican citizens of Texas look upon the Rangers, Mr. Canales said: "I wish to say that we believe the Texas Ranger force is an element of safety in the enforcement of laws if such force can be kept free from politics as the original force was; but it is a dangerous element and a menace to the citizens if the Ranger force is used for political purposes by the governor as it was used by Governor Hobby and Governor Ferguson." (Ibid., p. 515)

The ultimate result of the investigation was the law of March 31, 1919, which reduced the Ranger force to four regular companies not exceeding fifteen privates, a sergeant, and a captain. In addition, there was to be a headquarters company of six men under the charge of a senior captain. A sixth officer with the rank and pay of captain was to serve as quartermaster. The law also provided that any citizen could make a complaint against a Ranger for any offense and instructed the adjutant general to investigate the charge and institute legal action if the evidence warranted (ibid., p. 516). The bill in effect retired the Texas Rangers as the principal state police force.

After the Canales investigation, the Texas Rangers were not as prominent in state law enforcement, but the reorganization of the force was not successful. "Prohibition laws brought even further decline in public respect. Officers faced charges of theft, embezzlement, homicide, gaming, and other types of misconduct" (Prassel, 1972, p. 159). Webb notes that local law enforcement officers often resented the raids made by the Rangers in their jurisdiction (Webb, 1935, p. 513). Apparently the Rangers were also active in San Antonio in this type of activity. The December 14, 1924, issue of the *San Antonio Express* notes that Rangers helped in arresting moonshiners.

The San Antonio city elections of 1923 took an interesting turn when a front page headline story in the *San Antonio Light* alleged that supporters of the Citizens' Ticket, headed by L. B. Stoner, had asked that Texas Rangers be sent to the city for the elections. The newspaper story noted:

> Just what object the supporters of the Citizens' Ticket expect to accomplish by bringing Rangers here could not be determined Saturday. The primary election, it was pointed out, was conducted in a clean and orderly manner and required very little supervision from county and city officers. It is generally believed that the action of the Stoner supporters in attempting to bring Rangers here will serve to materially discredit the ticket. At the same time reports of the request for Rangers were circulated Thursday, it was also reported that attempts might be made to intimidate the negro and Mexican voters. (May 5, 1923, p. 1)

Sheriff John Tobin, running for mayor on an opposing ticket, denied that it was he who had asked for the Rangers, and Tobin scored a resounding victory.

A footnote in the case worthy of mention is that Tobin resigned as sheriff on May 31, 1923, to accept the office of mayor the following day (*San Antonio Express,* June 1, 1923, p. 11). In the transcript of the *Elgin v. Neff* case, it was reported that the Rangers "on or about" June 1, 1923, established headquarters for a Ranger company in San Antonio with B. C. Baldwin in charge (*Elgin* v. *Neff,* 1925, p. 13). June 1, 1923, is the day that Tobin became mayor of San Antonio.

Webb relates the story of a visit he made in a Model T Ford to Ranger headquarters in San Antonio in 1924 with Captain R. W. Aldrich, quartermaster of the force. Webb states:

> Our first objective was San Antonio, where we found some thirty Rangers in the charge of Captain B. C. Baldwin. Governor Pat Neff had sent the Rangers to San Antonio for the purpose of stopping liquor traffic and other infractions of the law. The political element in San Antonio resented the presence of the Rangers and fought bitterly to have them removed, but Governor Neff, equally stubborn, maintained them.

These men were quartered in an old residence at 331 Garden Street, south of the Alamo. On the whole they appeared to be the biggest men I had ever seen in one group, and they were about the most miserable. They spent their time between liquor raids in skylarking, a gay mask behind which to hide their longing for the home ranges. (Webb, 1935, p. 551)

Establishment of the Ranger headquarters in San Antonio sparked the process that lead to the *Elgin* v. *Neff* case. The plaintiff in the case was John E. Elgin, a private citizen described as a resident, taxpayer, and property owner of Bexar County. Elgin was concerned with the way tax funds were being spent and feared the Rangers were becoming an uncontrollable state police force. Elgin's petition declared that the law providing for the Texas Rangers was unconstitutional.

The defendants in the case included Pat Neff, governor of Texas; Lon A. Smith, comptroller of public accounts of Texas; C. V. Terrell, state treasurer; Thomas D. Barton, adjutant general of the state; B. W. Aldrich, quartermaster, commissary and paymaster of the Ranger force in Texas; and B. C. Baldwin, captain of the Ranger company in San Antonio (*Elgin* v. *Neff*, 1925, p. 1).

In the petition for injunction, Elgin asserted that the Texas Ranger law of 1919 was in violation of the Texas Constitution and that funding for Ranger operations should immediately cease. The court transcript refers to the possibility that Elgin was not acting alone, but had entered the suit in cooperation with several other persons. The petition states:

Plaintiff alleges that he is a property owner and tax paying citizen of the State of Texas, and a resident of Bexar County, and has been a property owner in said State for many years, including the years 1923 and 1924, and his property is now and will be subject to taxation, and that he will continue to pay State and County taxes for the purposes fixed by the Constitution and laws of Texas. That these taxes, so paid, and to be paid, by him, mingled with those of thousands of other citizens and taxpayers, have been received and will come into the Treasury of the State of Texas, and by reason thereof he has an interest in the manner in which the funds of the state are disbursed, and being so interested brings this suit for himself and all others similarly situated, and to prevent a multiplicity of suits to prevent such unlawful diversion of said public funds. (*Elgin* v. *Neff*, 1925, p. 18)

The petition summarized the 1919 Ranger law. It also cited sixteen specific points in conflict with the Texas Constitution, among these being Section 1 of the Bill of Rights, reserving to the people of Texas the right of local self-government, and the right to elect their own officers. The petition also cited nineteen reasons why the Ranger law should be declared void.

Some allegations in the petitions are especially interesting to note in detail:

1. Elgin asserted that the Ranger force was brought to Bexar County "without the request of the duly constituted officers charged with the enforcement of the law in said County, and that said force has been and is now kept and maintained in said County over the protest of said officers, at great expense to the taxpayers of Texas and without color of authority so to do" (ibid., p. 14). (Adjutant General Mark McGee also indicated later that the Rangers had been brought to Bexar County without the request of local lawmen.)

2. Elgin claimed that the Ranger company was not a militia of the state, as authorized by the constitution, but "on the contrary is a State Police Force" (ibid., p. 13).

3. Elgin also claimed that the sheriff and constables of Bexar County—as in the case of other counties—were under the Fee Bill, receiving their pay from fees taken in by them as lawmen. Fees over a certain amount reverted to the state and became public funds. Elgin claimed that Ranger activity in the Bexar County area was resulting in a lowering of the fees taken in by the lawmen, resulting in an increase in the burden on the taxpayers (ibid., pp. 17–18). In effect, Elgin was claiming that Ranger activities in the county were resulting in local lawmen losing their source of income.

The central theme of the petition was that the Rangers were operating through a law that was unconstitutional. The main contention concerning unconstitutionality was that the 1919 law created a state police force which was under command of the governor and *that the constitution not only forbade this, but assured citizens the right to have locally elected officials to enforce the laws.* The petition requested an injunction against the defendants to stop them from carrying out the provisions of House Bill 5, the law which amended the Ranger law. It was further asked that the 1919 act be declared invalid.

On August 2, 1924, Judge R. B. Minor refused to grant a temporary injunction in the case. He held that the case was too serious to grant a writ without a hearing. The hearing was set for October 20 (*San Antonio Express,* August 3, 1924, p. 6) but was delayed until December 1, 1924. Legal maneuverings included statements of the defendants which challenged the jurisdiction of the court, as the governor of the state was involved. Others noted that the state was ultimately involved in the case and that it had not consented to the suit.

Judge Minor took up the case on December 1, 1924, after all parties had waived having a jury. On January 15, 1925, the court ruled in favor of Elgin, enjoining all defendants except Governor Neff from paying Rangers' salaries and from paying for Ranger equipment.

The *San Antonio Express* noted at length:

> The court's ruling was said by attorneys on both sides to abolish the Ranger service which has been in existence in some form since the days of the Texas Republic. Although the court held he found no fault with the laws governing the Rangers previous to the statute of 1901, that the different statutes are so blended and interwoven that it would be impossible to separate them and the entire fabric must fall because of the void statutes giving Rangers authority in conflict with sheriffs and other county peace officers.
>
> If the writ is held to be operative at once, it will mean that Rangers must immediately cease their operations, and State

officials will be perpetually enjoined from paying salaries or disbursing money of the State toward the upkeep of the service.

Gov. Neff alone of all the parties made defendants was not enjoined, the court specially excepting the Governor from the operation of the order. . . .

Judge Minor held the law in violation of three articles of the State Constitution. . . .

The history of Ranger legislation in Texas was also reviewed and the court held that he found no fault with the law of 1877 adopted soon after the present Constitution was ratified. The Ranger force under that law was a strictly military organization organized for the purpose of protecting the frontier and was given no authority to serve criminal process and to act as peace officers in several counties of the State.

. . . The act of 1901 and amended in 1919 conferred upon members of the Ranger force the authority to serve criminal process in the counties of the sheriffs and constables, it was held. Sheriffs and constables alone have this power, the court declared, and any act of the Legislature in which it is attempted to confer those powers upon others is void. . . .

In speaking of the Governor's right to call out the militia in times of riot and other extreme cases, the court pointed out that when this is done the National Guard must act in conjunction with the local civil authorities and be under authority of the civil officers, while Rangers under the present law take orders from their own superior officers alone.

"The acts of the Legislature of 1901 and 1919 sought to create under another name a new body of sheriffs," said the court, "to act anywhere in the State. This is a plain assumption of the duties of the sheriffs of the State. No statute can be allowed to control when it is plainly in violation of the Constitution of the State. Violations of the Constitution can not be condoned nor permitted to continue."

Judge Minor further held that the creation of the Ranger force with powers of county police officers was in violation of the right of the people of the counties to name their own officers through elections.

. . . Judge Minor . . . reviewed the history of the adoption of the State Constitution, pointing out that the people of the State had just been freed from the oppression of a State officer under the carpetbag rule and that it would be irrational to think they would consider placing in the hands of the Governor so powerful a body as the present Ranger force. (January 16, 1925, p. 7)

Following the granting of the injunction, Assistant Attorney General W. A. Wheeler moved that its implementation be suspended pending appeal. Two days later, however, Judge Minor refused to suspend operation of the writ, ruling that it would remain in effect until some action was taken by the Fourth Court of Civil Appeals.

The judge's decision proved disastrous to the Texas Rangers. It meant that state officials were restrained from recognizing the Ranger force and could not pay the men. The Rangers were facing weeks, and perhaps even months, of being inactive and without pay. The *San Antonio Express* reported:

Capt. B. C. Baldwin in command of the company stationed in San Antonio is out of the city, it was announced at ranger headquarters, but men at the camp stated that the decision of Judge Minor would completely disrupt the service. The men said they could not afford to remain idle waiting on the case to drag its length through the courts and that they were all open to new jobs. (January 18, 1925, p. 1)

In overruling the motion to suspend operation of the permanent injunction grant, Judge Minor noted he had examined other cases, but seriously doubted the court's jurisdiction to suspend the operation of the injunction. He also added, "I am not satisfied that such a suspension would not deprive the decree of its finality" (*Elgin* v. *Neff*, 1925, p. 3).

Apparently the importance of the case caused the Fourth Court of Civil Appeals in San Antonio to immediately hear the appeal. On February 25, 1925, slightly more than a month after Minor's decision, Judge W. S. Fly, chief justice of the appeals court dissolved the injunction. Judge Fly reversed the ruling of the district court and dismissed the case. In summarizing the decision of the appellate, the *San Antonio Express* noted:

> The Court of Appeals in effect held that the law did not abridge the powers of other peace officers, but that the force was intended as an aid to such officers. The opinion pointed out that there have been cases where the powers of the Rangers have been abused and that some members of the force have performed unlawful acts, but that the court had nothing to do with that, the only question up for review being the constitutionality of the law.
>
> Chief Justice Fly reviewed in his opinion the entire history of the Ranger force, pointing out that the Rangers have been in existence since before the Republic of Texas. Many Legislatures since then have recognized the Rangers, by amending the law, adding to and decreasing the force and changing the status of the men and officers, he pointed out. . . .
>
> The State Legislature has all power which is not denied it by the Constitution, it was pointed out, and clearly has the authority to enact any law which is not plainly prohibited by the Constitution. No where in the Constitution is the creation of the Ranger force prohibited, it was held. (February 26, 1925, p. 11)

Although the Civil Appeals Court reversed the decision, the month during which the injunction was in force put into motion certain changes and alterations in the Ranger force. The *Express* story also noted the following changes in the Rangers, as a result of the court action:

1. Adjutant General Mark McGee announced in Austin that the dissolution of the injunction would have no effect on plans already made for removal of the Rangers from San Antonio. "McGee said it had already been decided to withdraw the State police from San Antonio, and the general policy not to send Rangers to any county without requests from local authorities will be adhered to" (ibid.).

2. A reorganization of the Ranger force would take place. The story noted that the force had already been reduced by

discharging twenty-eight men (ibid.). It was announced that there might be an increase in the size of the force if the state would appropriate the necessary funding. When Minor granted the injunction the Ranger force had included about one hundred men (*San Antonio Express*, January 18, 1925, p. 1). Discharge of twenty-eight men meant a significant reduction in the force.

In its February 26 issue the *Express* carried the report that Judge Fly of the Fourth Court of Civil Appeals had reversed Minor's decision. Ironically, on the front page of that same issue of the newspaper appeared another story that told of a severe rebuke given the Ranger force by a grand jury in Alpine that had been reviewing Ranger activities there. The story quoted the following from the grand jury report:

> We [the grand jury] respectfully request that you [the presiding judge] transmit to her excellency the Governor of Texas, Mrs. Miriam A. Ferguson, the unanimous recommendation of this body that in the future when Rangers are stationed in Brewster County, if any be so stationed—and we do not think any are needed—that they be instructed and cautioned in the authority which they have and in the powers that may be lawfully exercised by them in the discharge of the purpose for which they may be sent.
>
> This recommendation is deemed highly advisable for the reason that testimony has been submitted to the effect that in several instances Rangers Arch Miller and John Hollis have, wholly without authority and not in the line of duty, forcibly taken guns away from Mexicans then engaged in peaceable occupations and in no manner violating the law or even suspected of so doing, and then the Rangers summarily destroyed such property by breaking same to pieces on rocks.
>
> We deprecate such conduct, which is unjustifiable in law and reason, and while we have been unable to discover any conditions of affairs or lawlessness which warrants the presence of Rangers in the county, if they must be stationed here, we urge that they, too, be cautioned and required to obey the same laws which ostensibly they seek to enforce. (*San Antonio Express*, February 26, 1925, p. 1)

Although the guiding theme of the *Elgin* v. *Neff* case had been a fear that the mistakes of the Reconstruction years would be repeated and Texas would have a state police force, the case proved to be a landmark in the legislative history of the Texas Rangers. Both the Canales hearings and *Elgin* v. *Neff* presented another view of the Rangers during the first half of the twentieth century when the popular view was that of the "super-lawmen" fighting for justice on the side of law and order. The publicity given the Canales hearings and the lawsuit filed by Elgin showed the twentieth-century Texan that others besides outlaws had good reason to fear the Rangers. In addition, *Elgin* v. *Neff* set a precedent for the legal cases of the 1970s, when the Texas Rangers again found themselves defendants in court cases.

Get Your Man
and Keep No Records

IN JANUARY 1935 Governor James V. Allred began to make good his campaign promises of the previous year to overhaul the state's law enforcement machinery, and the Texas legislature approved a bill creating the Department of Public Safety. The much-needed reform of the Texas Rangers was implemented on October 7, 1935, when Governor Allred met with his Public Safety Commissioners to formulate Ranger policies. By the time of their reorganization the Texas Rangers had become wholly inadequate for the task of statewide law enforcement. The state had changed dramatically since the first "ranging men" rode the frontier; the Rangers, however, remained essentially unchanged. A report prepared in 1933 for the Texas legislature stated:

> From its inception, the policies of the Ranger force have been the same, and these are now accepted as traditional. These policies are in effect "Get your man and keep no records except of final results." (Report of the Joint Legislative Committee, 1933, p. 54)

While these policies were practiced in the days of the wholesale slaughter of Indians and Mexicans, it was becoming clear that killing all the Mexicans and driving all the Indians north of the Red River would not solve the Texas law enforcement problem. The state was no longer a frontier; by 1930 there were nearly six million people in Texas, more than 40 percent of them in urban areas. The state needed a statewide police force with systematic and scientific procedures for collecting and analyzing evidence, and the Texas Rangers were still relying on methods developed during the days of the frontier. Random executions of suspects—killed while trying to escape—very often left the real criminals at large.

> [Texas's] sister states must wonder whether such a reputation [one riot, one Ranger] is merited when notorious criminals can roam vast areas of the state robbing, killing, and kidnapping as they go for months on end without being apprehended.
>
> Explaining the stagnation of state police force activities is simple. Texas is trying to fight modern criminals with obsolete and outmoded police methods. (Fidler, 1935, p. 66)

Before the 1935 reorganization of the Rangers, the force had been embroiled in politics and had been used as pawns by the state's governors. In 1932 the Texas Rangers were very involved in the political sense, openly supporting Governor Ross Sterling for reelection. His opponent was Miriam A. Ferguson, whose husband, former Governor James E. Ferguson, had used the Texas Rangers "as currency to pay political debts, as a cheap method of elevating aspiring Texans to state peerage, as a kind of exclusive club for political hacks and cronies of the governor. . . . sometimes a Ranger commission became a license to rob or kill" (Proctor, 1970, p. 213). (The force did include some outstanding lawmen like Captain Frank Hamer, who, after resigning his Ranger commission, tracked down Clyde Barrow and Bonnie Parker.) When newly elected Governor Miriam Ferguson moved to Austin in January 1933, those in the Ranger force who had not already resigned were discharged, and, it has been noted:

> once again the Texas Rangers were a source of patronage, corruption, and ridicule. The effect upon state law enforcement was, of course, catastrophic. During the next two years crime and violence became widespread, bank holdups and murder commonplace. (Ibid., p. 214)

Mrs. Ferguson issued more than 2,300 special Ranger commissions, with some going to former convicts (Prassel, 1972, p. 158). During her incumbency, "special" Ranger commissions "became badges of dishonor and objects of derision. One of the large newspapers stated, 'A Ranger Commission and a nickel will get you a cup of coffee anywhere in Texas' " (Sterling, 1959, p. 519).

The Rangers Reorganized

Under the 1935 law that created the Department of Public Safety, Governor Allred appointed a three-man Public Safety Commission, which set higher standards for the Rangers. Examinations, recommendations, seniority, and performance became the criteria for appointment and promotion. The Commission made provisions for the Rangers to be instructed in modern techniques of crime detection. The state was divided into five, and then six, districts in which a Ranger company was given specific responsibility and jurisdiction. Each company was composed of a captain, a sergeant, and a number of privates.

The Public Safety Commissioners selected a director and an assistant director to head the Department of Public Safety. The department was then set up under three distinct units—the Texas Rangers, the Texas Highway Patrol, and the new Headquarters Division at Austin, which was a scientific crime laboratory and detection center. The role of the Texas Rangers in state law enforcement was greatly reduced. Prior to this time they were the only state police force in Texas, as the State Highway Patrol had lacked full police powers. Mounted on motorcycles, the Highway Patrol had enforced only traffic and vehicle control laws. Like the Rangers, they had no crime laboratory, no radio communications system, no record-keeping facilities for cataloguing data about criminals, such as fingerprints. The new Department of Public Safety law bolstered the Texas Highway Patrol by giving it all the powers previously given only to Texas Rangers. The ranks of the Highway Patrol were increased to 147 men, with more to be added in 1936. The number of Rangers was maintained at thirty-six men.

Under the new law the Texas Rangers were transferred from the adjutant general's office to the Department of Public Safety. The new law and the policies set up by the Public Safety Commissioners stabilized the Ranger force. The customary two-year appointments to the force made by each new governor had led to a disastrously politicized corps. Since the captains especially were apt to be replaced by a new governor there had been virtually no continuity in the force. This proved to be more than normally disruptive, as most of the collected information about criminal activities in the state had been deposited in the memories of both current and former Rangers. The first director of the Department of Public Safety, L. G. Phares, changed the Ranger habit of keeping few records of their activities by requiring weekly written reports of all Texas Rangers.

In January 1935 Governor Allred ordered Adjutant General Carl Nesbitt to revoke all the "special" Ranger commissions, estimated at over two thousand. The law creating the Department of Public Safety, which became effective on August 10, 1935, limited the number of such commissions to 300. Special Rangers were authorized to enforce only those laws of the state designed to protect life and property. Special Rangers had no connection with a regular Ranger company or uniformed unit of the Department of Public Safety; they received no compensation from the state; and they were required to enter into a $2,500 bond indemnifying all persons against damages accruing as a result of illegal acts on their part. Despite the modernization of the force, many special Rangers continued to be employed by Texas cowmen, oil companies, and other vested interests.

Important as the steps taken to improve the quality of the Rangers were, state law enforcement as a whole profited more from the creation of the Headquarters Division at Austin. The Headquarters Division was composed of four bureaus: Identification and Records, Intelligence, Communications, and Education. With the establishment of the Headquarters Division, the state finally had the means to fashion a modern, efficient law enforcement body.

Under the Headquarters Division, the Bureau of Identification and Records functioned as a central file of photographs, fingerprints, and other data on felons convicted in Texas after 1935. Ballistics and laboratory work were included in this bureau. The Bureau of Intelligence collected information on criminal *modus operandi,* and the Bureau of Communications established a statewide police radio network. One of the responsibilities of the bureau was to coordinate with local law enforcement agencies. The Bureau of Education was responsible for training all new officers in the Department of Public Safety and for conducting specialized training courses for county and municipal law enforcement officers.

Although formally established in one division of the Department of Public Safety, all four bureaus were hindered from complete development for several years because of a lack of funds, facilities, and personnel. Responsibilities were shared within the division and, in situations where special equipment and/or trained personnel were not available, assistance was provided by local law enforcement agencies, the Texas Public Health Service, or the University of Texas.

While the Texas Highway Patrol became the preeminent force in state law enforcement because of their numerical superiority (e.g., in 1937 the Texas Highway Patrol numbered 236 men, while there were fewer than forty Texas Rangers), the Texas Rangers did not die out as some had feared and others had hoped. The duties of the Texas Rangers did not change substantially after the organization of the Department of Public Safety. Rangers continued to enforce the state's gambling and narcotics laws. The force's criminal investigations centered around such major crimes as murder, rape, assault, robbery, burglary, and theft of livestock. However, Rangers were no longer seen "guarding" polls during elections.

By 1938 the Texas Rangers were serving under the third head of the Department of Public Safety. L. G. Phares had served only eight months as acting director and director of the Department of Public Safety. He was replaced in May 1936 by Colonel Horace H. Carmichael, who was a veteran of World War I and had served for ten years as assistant adjutant general for the state of Texas. Following Colonel Carmichael's death in September 1938, Assistant Director Homer Garrison, Jr., became acting director and was named to succeed Carmichael. Garrison had been assistant director of the Department of Public Safety since its inception in 1935 and he was to serve as its director for thirty years until his death in 1968. Eleven days after Garrison's appointment as director, Ranger Captain S. O. Hamm became the new assistant director.

Fighting Germans and Communists

In 1941, when the United States entered World War II, the thirty-five members of the Texas Rangers were called on to deal with aliens of German and Japanese nationality and with thousands of United States citizens in Texas who were unfortunate enough to have German ancestors. The Texas Rangers and the Texas Department of Public Safety joined the FBI and the U.S. Immigration Service in investigating and policing suspected enemy sympathizers. Three detention camps were set up for those aliens in Texas deemed poor security risks. But even with the twenty-nine prisoner-of-war camps established in the state, anti-German feeling never ran so high as it had during the First World War. During World War I persons suspected of sympathy with the Germans were picked up by the Rangers on the most trivial of charges: "All who bore a German name or spoke with a German accent were suspects, and if one expressed sympathy for Germany, the government agents were sure to be upon him" (Webb, 1935, p. 506).

Also during the 1930s, the Rangers came to grips with the "Red Menace." The most publicized of the Ranger captains, Frank Hamer, sent agents to infiltrate Communist organizations in Texas. When Hamer received word that oil reserves in both Texas and Oklahoma were going to be sabotaged, Hamer warned the oil companies to double their guard. When dynamite was stolen in Oklahoma, a local police chief released Hamer's letter and the Communists went into hiding (Frost and Jenkins, 1968, pp. 169–170).

When the United States once again faced the German menace in World War II, Texas Rangers were again called on to aid in the case of internal national defense. Colonel Garrison put Ranger Captain N. K. Dixon on the job of investigating German aliens in Texas. Escaped German prisoners of war were tracked down by Rangers using bloodhounds, horses, and automobiles equipped with two-way radios. The Rangers' and highway patrolmen's knowledge of the local terrain was of valuable assistance to military units searching for escapees. Improved relations with Mexico kept Texas's long international border, a potential trouble spot, relatively quiet (Webb, unpublished ms., ch. 24, revision of *The Texas Rangers*). Texas Rangers toured the state showing films to persons training to be air raid wardens; Rangers, Texas highway patrolmen, and FBI agents made raids on the homes of aliens in which they seized firearms and short-wave radios; and aliens of questionable loyalty were arrested and placed in detention camps.

The Rangers Up to Date

By the end of the war, the Texas Rangers had undergone several changes. In order to provide closer supervision of the force, the Rangers were directly responsible to the director of the Department of Public Safety, and the state legislature had increased the force to forty-five men. The legislature was giving the Department of Public Safety more substantial appropriations for more equipment and better training to meet modern law enforcement problems, and the increased funding was felt in all divisions. Training for both Rangers and highway patrolmen improved.

In 1947 the Ranger force was increased to fifty-one men. The Bureau of Communication finally received funds and authorization for a statewide radio communications system. The legislature approved a bill in 1949 which authorized the construction of new headquarters for the Department of Public Safety. When the department moved into its new headquarters in 1953 and 1954, all branches were, for the first time, housed under one roof. In 1949 the department bought an airplane, and Max Westerman became the first Ranger pilot-investigator. Westerman distinguished himself when he captured a fleeing arsonist by landing the Department of Public Safety airplane on the highway in front of the speeding fugitive. Although there were occasional heroics like Westerman's feat, the vast majority of Ranger work was in routine criminal investigations in conjunction with local law enforcement officers. Rangers enforced gambling laws, and from 1939 when Governor W. Lee O'Daniel vetoed the Bureau of Narcotics appropriation, to 1953 when the appropriation reappeared, a few Rangers enforced narcotics laws.

Thus the history of the Texas Rangers as a distinct unit becomes increasingly difficult to follow after the reorganization of Texas law enforcement in 1935. From 1935, when the Rangers came under the jurisdiction of the Department of Public Safety, to the present, their legality and function have continued to be questioned. While the Rangers and highway patrolmen remain separate units, their powers as state law enforcement officers are essentially the same. Rangers generally do not concern themselves with traffic control, but highway patrolmen do conduct criminal investigations. In cases of disaster, both Rangers and highway patrolmen are available to assist local law enforcement officials in rescue efforts or in maintaining order. In Austin the Headquarters Division, the central laboratory and training headquarters, is manned by men from both divisions. This duplication of function is one reason, among many, that is advanced when the abolition of the Texas Rangers is urged. As one commentator has said:

> The Texas Rangers ought to be abolished as an outfit and the Rangers transferred into the Department of Public Safety's corps of officers. The Rangers are, no doubt, a tourist attraction, but they serve no proper distinctive function, and they have come for various reasons, many of them legitimate, to symbolize the oppression of Mexican-Americans and, more recently, farm workers. (Dugger, *Texas Observer,* May 9, 1969, p. 3)

A May 1955 incident led the Department of Public Safety to purchase a fleet of five M-8 light armored vehicles. N. J. Tynes, suspected of shooting an eighteen-year-old boy, barricaded himself inside his farmhouse. His skill with a rifle and the open fields surrounding his house made Tynes's capture difficult. Ranger Captain Clint Peoples solved the problem by borrowing an armored vehicle from nearby Fort Hood. The Rangers used the military vehicle to pump tear gas shells into the house, and Tynes was mortally wounded during his capture. Following this incident, the Department of Public Safety purchased five of the armored cars equipped with turrets, shortwave radios, riot guns, and tear gas. The vehicles were stationed around the state and kept in readiness.

By 1957, after more than twenty years of operations and piecemeal additions, the Department of Public Safety's original organizational lines had become blurred and confused. Some areas of responsibility were duplicated and others neglected as additional tasks were added. In 1957 the Department of Public Safety reorganized the Headquarters Division and divided the state into six regional commands to supervise the 570 highway patrolmen. By 1959 there were nearly nine hundred patrolmen.

The Texas Rangers, however, were not included in the regional reorganization. They continued to be directly responsible to the director of the Department of Public Safety. For convenience, each of the six Ranger company headquarters was located in the same city as the department's regional headquarters. Thus, since 1957 Ranger companies have been headquartered at Corpus Christi, Dallas, Houston, Lubbock, Midland, and Waco. By 1964 the number of Texas Rangers had increased to sixty-two. By 1973 there were eighty-two Rangers and the legislature had authorized twelve more positions in the force to be added over the next two years.

Senior Ranger Captain Bill Wilson sees the modern-day Texas Rangers as part of the history and heritage of the Lone Star State, but he adds: "We're not trying to live on our past heritage. We're trying to do a job for the people of Texas that they're paying for" (interview, Ann Fears Crawford with Captain W. D. Wilson, Ranger Headquarters, Austin, February 4, 1976). He sees the Rangers' work as one part of the Department of Public Safety and within the jurisdiction of the department. According to Captain Wilson, there are ninety-four Rangers serving within the state's six districts, and decentralized from the Ranger Headquarters in Austin. Each of the six districts covers an assigned area from one to six counties, depending upon the size of the county and the amount of work to be done. Each district is under the supervision of a captain and a sergeant, with an average of twelve to thirteen Rangers assigned to a district. The largest district has a total of sixteen Rangers (ibid.).

The Department of Public Safety sets the pay scale for the Rangers. Senior captains receive $20,340 a year; assistant supervisors, $18,420; captains $17,244; sergeants, $14,628; and the Rangers, $13,248. The Rangers must buy their own uniforms, boots, and hats—just as the frontier "ranging men" had to supply their own clothing.

Captain Wilson is well aware of the criticism that the Texas Rangers have received during the past few years. However, he feels that the Rangers have done a good job and have done the job that the people of Texas want done. In answering queries about the Rangers' conflicts with the Mexican Americans in the Rio Grande valley, Captain Wilson responded: "Somebody on one side always accuses you of favoring the other side" (ibid).

During the 1960s and 1970s the Texas Rangers were once again under investigation because of their interference in the elections in Crystal City in 1963 and their abuse of power during the farmworkers' strike in 1966 and 1967. These topics are discussed in chapters seven and eight.

Los Cinco Candidatos

THE EVOLUTION OF the role of the Texas Rangers from Indian fighters to guardians of an exclusionary political process came to national attention in 1963 by way of Crystal City, Texas.

Crystal City lies in the center of Texas's Zavala County, 120 miles south of San Antonio and some fifty miles from the Rio Grande. Although it is surrounded by the flat, sparsely populated brush country of South Texas, Zavala County is the heart of the Texas Winter Garden area. Its fertile soil, mild winters, and capacity for extensive irrigation provide growers with crops the year round. The self-proclaimed "Spinach Capital of the World," Crystal City has earned its title by producing 80 percent of the total spinach crop grown in the United States (*Chicano Almanac*, 1973, p. 240). Evidence of pride in that fact can be found in the town square, where one of the largest producers has erected a ten-foot-high statue of Popeye.

Agriculture and its related businesses form the economic base of Crystal City; and planting, harvesting, field packing, and canning of spinach, onions, cabbage, carrots, cantaloupe, and watermelon form the county's major industry. The fields, packing sheds, canneries, and profits are dominated by a combination of local Anglo growers and the Del Monte Corporation, the largest single producer and employer in the area. The backbreaking field harvesting, the long hours spent packing and canning the crops for distribution, and the low seasonal wages are the total domain of the more fortunate Mexican Americans. They are fortunate because they work and because, no matter how low the wages, they make money. This is an important factor in a community where the yearly unemployment rate averages 12 percent. Of the county's work force of 5,650 persons, approximately 1,500, or 26 percent, are agricultural workers.

Few people live well in Crystal City, but those who do are Anglo. Even so, only 3.7 percent of the families—all Anglo—have a median income of $10,000 or above. The large majority of Mexican Americans earn much less. In the total distribution of income throughout Texas, 28.7 percent of the state's total population is included in the $1,000 to $2,999 income bracket, well below the national poverty level. In Zavala County, 63.5 percent of the residents fall within the $1,000 to $2,999 income bracket.

In view of these statistics, it is not surprising that out of 3,544 houses in the county, only 800 houses have cold running water inside, 900 houses have water available from outside faucets, and occupants of 252 homes have no water at all on their premises. These last must go to the City Service Center to buy their water by the gallon. Nor are the educational statistics surprising—median school years completed by Mexican-American males average 3.0 grades, and slightly higher, 5.2 grades, for Anglo males.

The pervasive poverty of the area, heightened by the seasonal work period, forces more than 3,000 Mexican-American agricultural workers to follow the migrant stream each year to find work in the agricultural fields of other states. The migrant exodus usually begins in April, with workers returning to their homes in Crystal City in September to work the winter garden crops.

Prior to 1962 no one questioned the pattern of life in Crystal City—a life characterized by the hard edge of poverty, unalleviated by low educational attainment, little economic opportunity, and nonexistent political choice. The political power of the community—school board, school system, city and county offices, and law enforcement—was firmly entrenched among a handful of Anglos, elected by the 14.5 percent Anglo population of Crystal City. In 1959 and preceding years, Mexican Americans only accounted for 10 to 15 percent of the voters registered in Crystal City, although they comprised 85 percent of the town's population. The political decision-making by the long-term Anglo office holders (until 1963 the mayor of Crystal City had served continuously for thirty-eight years; each of the five city councilmen had served for over thirty-eight years) was more akin to the "divine right of kings" than to a democratic electoral process. Through the seeming complaisance of the predominant Mexican-American population the idea was perpetuated that only Anglos were fit to hold office or other responsible positions in the community.

In Crystal City, although poverty is common to both Anglos and Mexican Americans, the unification of the Anglo community was based on feelings of ethnic superiority, reinforced by those sworn to uphold the law. The main thrust of law enforcement came thorugh the Texas Rangers based in nearby Carrizo Springs. Under the direction of Captain A. Y. Allee, the Rangers who lived in the area were on close and friendly terms with officeholders in the community. When a disturbance of any nature broke out involving the Mexican-American population, it was not uncommon for the Rangers to come in to quell it. The Anglo community took it for granted that the Rangers were there to protect Anglo interests; no one ever accused the Rangers operating in South Texas of either upholding or enforcing the law impartially.

Captain A. Y. Allee—A Law unto Himself

Before we review the Crystal City events, it is appropriate to digress for a moment to give the reader a portrait of a modern Ranger who has earned a place of prominence in recent Ranger history and played a major role in Crystal City affairs.

Born in Encinal, Texas, on September 14, 1905, A. Y.

Allee served as a peace officer in Bee County before joining the Rangers on February 6, 1931. He left the Ranger service on January 18, 1933, and served as chief deputy officer of Bee County, until he rejoined the Ranger force on March 1, 1935, after which he served continuously until he retired on October 1, 1970.

Most of Allee's service was in the southern part of Texas, patrolling the Mexican border. On August 1, 1947 he was named acting captain of Company D; he was promoted to captain on September 1, 1957. After his retirement in 1970, Allee continued to be active in Ranger activities and was elected president of the Former Texas Rangers Association at the group's annual meeting in May 1971.

Allee was born and bred of Texas Ranger blood. His grandfather, Alfred Young Allee I, and his father, Lonzo Allee, had served with the Texas Rangers as commissioned, unpaid men who worked with the regular Rangers on call. Allee's son, Alfred Y. Alee, Jr., currently serves as a member of the Ranger force (Allee's cousin, Tom, was a Zavala County Commissioner who played a role in Allee's Rio Grande City enforcement in 1966–67.) ("Biographical Sketch Captain A. Y. Allee," Austin: Texas Rangers Headquarters, Texas Department of Public Safety, n.d.; also *San Antonio Express,* September 13, 1970, p. 2A).

The controversial Allee has been the subject of wide-ranging descriptions. Many people have noted that he was gruff and humorless; yet a *Dallas Morning News* story carried the headline "Allee Has Heart of Gold, Friends Say" *(Dallas Morning News,* July 9, 1967, p. 1), and the official Ranger biography of the captain notes

> He has been described by his friends as fearless, courageous, honest, kind and intelligent. He is respected and feared by those who break the law. Many citizens of South Texas have recognized his ability and dedication and have taken time to express their thoughts by submitting letters of appreciation. He is well known for having no fear. . . . ("Biographical Sketch," n.p.)

The plaintiff in one of several court cases against Allee, however, noted in his original petition:

> Defendant is a man given to sudden fits of anger and rage and has a quick, irascible and violent character and temperament. Defendant further has a notorious, well-known reputation and is known to have been frequently involved in allegations of mistreatment and brutality directed by him against persons of all ethnic backgrounds and races but particularly toward persons of Mexican descent. (*Lopez* v. *Allee,* 1972, p. 2)

On the eve of Allee's retirement the *San Antonio Express* ran a story reviewing his career, in which his wife stated that

> Captain Allee has spent much time with the youth of this state. Obviously there's no generation gap that deters the young from asking and accepting his advice . . . he has been instrumental in keeping many of all nationalities in school, helping others obtain jobs and helping some young married couples resolve their differences—and older ones, as far as that is concerned. (September 13, 1970, p. 2A)

The *Express* story also mentioned that Allee had been named in several lawsuits, and quoted the former Ranger captain as saying, "I don't regret anything I have done. In 44 years I have never been convicted of anything or lost any lawsuit." The news article also noted that Allee spoke both Spanish and English and that the Ranger captain considered that he treated both Mexican Americans and Anglos fairly. Allee is quoted as saying:

> A peace officer's job is not to put everybody in the pen, but to try to help straighten them up if they get out of line. To try to help them become good citizens. I've always tried to do that with Latins and whites both. (Ibid.)

Even after the captain retired from active service, he continued to be a controversial figure in South Texas. Someone once described Ranger Captain Allee's courage by stating, "He would charge Hell with a teaspoon of water" ("Biographical

Sketch," n.p.). Ironically, a confrontation in 1971 between Allee and Abel Lopez, Jr., which led to a lawsuit, centered around the price of a bottle of water.

It can be said unequivocably that Texas Ranger Allee lived up to the history of his predecessors.

Registering the Voters

In 1962 a young Chicano from Crystal City, Teamster's Union organizer Moses Falcón, appealed to Bexar County Commissioner Albert A. Peña, Jr., state chairman of the Political Association of Spanish Speaking Organizations (PASO), for help with a voter registration drive among Crystal City's Mexican-American population. That simple request set off a chain of events which vitally influenced the political awareness of Chicanos throughout Texas. On the surface, the education of American citizens in the democratic process is considered not only a right, but an obligation of every citizen. But in Crystal City, in 1962, it was considered revolution.

Leaders of PASO had been building up Mexican-American voting strength in Texas since the 1960 presidential campaign for John F. Kennedy. Albert Fuentes, PASO state executive secretary and a survivor of San Antonio's west-side political infighting, was fond of citing the potential political impact of Texas's two million Mexican Americans he habitually described as "the sleeping giant" (Larry Goodwyn, "Los Cinco Candidatos," *Texas Observer,* April 18, 1963, p. 3). Mexican-American power in San Antonio politics is a permanent fact of that city's life. However, Albert Peña stated that Mexican Americans as a political force were still laggard in Texas because of two factors: Mexican Americans were afraid they would lose their jobs if they stepped out politically, and they did not believe they had a chance to win against Anglo candidates.

The situation in Crystal City was ideal for a local test of

Mexican-American voting strength. Although Anglo-dominated, the town had a Mexican-American majority. In addition, a large number of the several hundred workers at the California Packing Co. (Del Monte) plant belonged to a local chapter of the Teamsters Union and were protected against political firings. The Teamsters and PASO, at Moses Falcón's request, joined in with a will on the poll tax drive, and at the end of January 1963 better than a two-to-one majority of the qualified voters were people with Spanish surnames.

For seven months, from the start of a voter registration drive in October until April, when the city election took place, the birth pangs of democracy in Crystal City were accompanied by newly aroused courage on the part of the Mexican Americans, which the Anglos met with fear, intimidation, harrassment, and the Texas Rangers.

Albert Fuentes went to Crystal City to help organize the voter registration drive. "The Teamsters were the only ones allowed to be deputized to get the poll tax books. For three years we had been registering voters this way, and the city administration wasn't concerned. However, cost of the tax—for a couple it was $3.50 at $1.75 each—was prohibitive. Many families did not earn that much in each week. They would bring nickels, dimes, and quarters over a period of weeks. We told the people the full amount had to be paid by January, or we'd give them their money back. The Rangers and the clerks watched carefully to see that we were not paying for poll taxes ourselves" (interview, Albert Peña with Albert Fuentes, San Antonio, May 23, 1973).

Henry Muñoz, an organizer for both the Teamsters Union and PASO, went to Crystal City with Teamster organizer Carlos Moore and found that the clerk in charge of the poll tax books refused to issue poll tax forms to Mexican Americans. "She said the migrants weren't reliable. She suspected they would leave town or pocket the money," Muñoz recalls (interview, Albert Peña with Henry Muñoz, San Antonio, March 16, 1973). In spite of the fact that migrants were citizens and were forced to seek work wherever they might find it, the clerk expressed prejudicial rationales for refusing to carry out her duties. "With these Mexicans," she told Muñoz, "it's easier to move out than pay the rent" (ibid.). The books eventually passed over to the Chicano registers, after the clerk warned them that the Texas Rangers would apprehend anyone out of line and would jail them for stealing money from the county.

"In October, after the drive started and the word was out that Carlos and I were registering Chicanos," Muñoz recalled, "we were put out of the hotel by the hotel management. That same day we were summoned to the mayor's office where four Rangers, including Captain A. Y. Allee and Sergeant Jack Van Cleave, waited for us. Allee spoke for the group and told us we were troublemakers and to get the hell out of town" (ibid.).

In spite of the Ranger's threats, the drive continued. Fuentes recalls the drive's progress. "We pointed out unfair situations to people as we registered them to vote. Some situations were ridiculous. The Lions Club sponsored a troop of Boy Scouts for Anglos only, and they were much better equipped than the Mexican-American Scout troop. When questioned about the separation of the two troops, officials told us that the Mexican-American Scouts didn't take bread for sandwiches on hikes. They took tortillas instead and were embarrassed about it. That's why they kept the two troops separate. That sounds funny, but that's what the Scout officials told us" (interview, Fuentes).

Some situations were even more serious. Mexican Americans were charged excessive tax rates, with the city tax department keeping separate tax files, one for Anglos and one for Mexican Americans. The water department also kept separate records on Anglo- and Mexican-American customers. The records proving these charges exist on file with the United States Congress.

The use of the municipal swimming pool proved to be

another way the city used to humiliate and put down the Chicano, Muñoz recalls: "The swimming pool was cleaned on Thursdays, and Anglos had exclusive use of the pool on Friday, Saturday, and Sunday. Chicanos could use the pool on Monday, Tuesday, and Wednesday after the water was dirty. Many Chicanos said 'Well, we don't want to swim with the Anglos anyway,' but the issue was that Chicanos were only allowed in when the pool was dirty. The older Mexican Americans said that the situation had always been that way, and they could not see how the situation could change. However, they could see that although it was too late for them to go to a school of equal quality or to join the same Boy Scout troop, it was not too late for their children to have pride, dignity, and self-respect. And they began to think like equals and to put themselves in a position to participate on equal ground with Anglos" (interview, Muñoz).

As the Mexcian-American community became more aware of issues of equality, they began to see a reason to organize around a statewide political organization—PASO—which had broad-based state support for changing conditions. The issues also gave the people a reason for registering to vote and making the effort the most successful poll tax drive in the city's history. In 1951 Mexican Americans represented between 10 to 15 percent of the total voter registration. In 1960 Anglos had 683 poll taxes compared to 646 paid by those with Spanish surnames. In 1962 Anglo registration dropped to 538, and Mexican-American registration rose to 795. The year 1963 brought a sharp increase: Mexican-American registrations numbered 1,139 out of a total of 1,681. Eighty-five percent of the population had finally achieved an initial voting majority (Shockley, 1974, p. 26).

Up to this time, the city authorities and the Rangers had mainly restricted themselves to surveillance drives. Since there was little else to do, they checked on poll tax workers. When the registration figures were in, the city fathers faced a potentially serious electoral challenge. Judging by their later actions, the Rangers were provoked by the success of the drive and the challenge it presented.

Challenging the Council

Five days after the poll tax drive was completed, Martin García, a law student at St. Mary's University in San Antonio, moved to Crystal City to provide technical assistance to the newly registered voters. García lived with the residents in their homes and felt their fears until the campaign was over (Goodwyn, "Los Cinco Candidatos," p. 3). García recalls that he had the name of Juan Cornejo, the local Teamster business agent, to contact in Crystal City. "[Cornejo] suggested we go see a man named Andrew Dickens, who had been talking of starting a ticket to oppose the city council," García states (interview, Albert Peña with Martin García, Houston, June 12, 1973). Fuentes confirms that the initiative to field a slate of candidates began with an Anglo, Andrew Dickens. "Dickens was mad at Mayor B. H. Holsomback over the new property assessment on his doughnut shop. His motivation for fighting the incumbents was purely personal. He had warned the mayor that he would put together a ticket with three Mexicans on it to run against the incumbent council" (interview, Fuentes).

García found that Dickens was ineligible to run for office. "He was all excited about beating the hell out of the guys at city hall, but he lived outside the city limits. We had talked of a mixed slate; in terms of finding other Anglos in the community to form a representative slate. I found out later that it was an impossibility—nobody but Dickens, who had a grudge, would dare," says García (interview, García).

The Mexican Americans had been cut loose from their only Anglo backer to swim by themselves, or, better yet, to forget about the election. "We decided to search for candidates," García recalls. "I advised Juan Cornejo to talk to some of the Chicano businessmen about running on the ticket. I had in mind a Chicano who owned a supermarket" (ibid.). But fears of economic reprisals and troublesome administrative inspections kept the businessmen from filing for the race. "Everyone who had a little grocery store or a small business was simply scared, intimidated from the start," says Henry Muñoz. "When I talked with them, they said the city would jump in and send a building inspector to condemn their buildings and put them out of business. Or else the Texas Rangers would pay them a visit and talk things straight" (interview, Muñoz).

The Mexican-American businessmen's fears were founded on experience. Past challenges had been squelched through just these techniques. Their fear was real. It was not the city inspectors who were out to put them out of business, it was the city council, the Rangers, the city marshal, and the county sheriff.

"We began having open meetings in our search for candidates," García recalls. However, only twenty-three people came to the first meeting in early February. "I was depressed by the small number," García remembers, "considering Juan Cornejo was a business agent for the Teamsters, I thought for sure he would bring his membership. But there were others watching through the windows of the meeting hall and listening outside the door, all afraid to participate. Even though they had brought their poll taxes, the election process was strange to them" (interview, García).

All twenty-three men attending the first meeting became directors of the Citizens Committee for Better Government, and they made a decision to run five candidates in the April elections. Fuentes explained that the full five-man slate was dictated by the election methods of the Crystal City city council. "Our study showed that all power in Crystal City was vested in the five-man city council that hired the city manager. The election system used was primitive—the five with the highest votes won, with no runoffs," Fuentes recalls (interview, Fuentes).

"We reasoned that it would be possible for us to be totally shut out if we ran only two or three candidates. The Anglos could tell the voters, 'Go ahead and vote for Juan, Pedro, and Miguel; but don't forget your friends John and Sam. You've got five votes. Vote for your three, but vote for us also.' This approach sounds plausible, but by carefully blocking out his votes, and voting only for the Anglo candidates, the Anglo could still blow us off the ballot. In 'high-man-wins' politics, a Mexican American's own vote could help elect Anglos, since whoever had the most votes overall would win," Fuentes says (ibid.).

The citizens group understood the problem. "They agreed when we said that we had to run five Chicano candidates. The average voter would have thought that he could vote for John and Sam without hurting his candidates' chances, and with less than five on the ballot we would not be able to convince them otherwise. If the average voter knew there were five candidates on the ballot, he would know he could vote five times. The system had laid out our fundamental strategy for us with no chance for compromise," Fuentes says (ibid.).

Fifty persons attended the next meeting. Before the third meeting was to be held, the citizens committee rented a sound truck from San Antonio to cruise the city announcing the upcoming meeting. One hundred persons attended, and several different ad hoc neighborhood groups began backing slates of candidates. Anyone who wanted to run for the council was told to show up at the next meeting, where, according to García, the final five would be selected by the democratic process.

"At the next meeting," Fuentes recalls, "we got together and explained the technique of divide and conquer, where the opposing candidates would convince others to file and split the Anglo vote" (ibid.). García told the group that anyone who filed later, after not coming forward, would split the Mexican-American vote, dilute their strength, and probably get the Mexican-American slate beat. Not coming forward and putting his name in and subsequently running would be considered an act of treason.

Sixteen candidates were listed on a blackboard at the front of the meeting hall. According to the city charter, candidates had to hold poll taxes, own property, and be free of debt to the city. "After we measured the candidates against the qualifications," Fuentes recalls, "nine hopefuls were left. At the fourth meeting each of the nine stood up before the crowd, in front of the microphone, and gave his word of honor as a man that he would support the five candidates chosen" (ibid.). The five candidates chosen that night were: Juan Cornejo, the local Teamsters agent; Antonio Cárdenas, a truck driver for an oil company; Manuel Maldonado, a clerk for the Economart hardware store; Mario Hernández, a house salesman; and Reynaldo Mendoza, an operator of a small photography shop.

The Anglos Strike Back

"It was after this fourth meeting, when as a group we announced our candidates, that the obstructionism of the Anglo establishment began in earnest," García recalls. "The next morning we went down to file at city hall and came back empty-handed. The clerk told us there were no application forms for filing. A Chicana working in the courthouse passed us an old pamphlet with the charter in the back. A form was in an appendix. Using an old typewriter of Juan's, I typed out the forms one by one, without benefit of carbon paper. It took us five hours. We found a notary who sold houses to notarize the forms. Mendoza, who owned the photography shop, took pictures so we would have visual proof that we had actually filed" (interview, García).

The city hall crowd had never seen Mexican Americans so "arrogant" before. But on Wednesday the Crystal City newspaper acknowledged that the five candidates, *los cinco can-*

didatos, had duly filed (Goodwyn, "Los Cinco Candidatos,"
p. 4).

Incidents of brute intimidation began to parallel incidents
of obstructionism. "In March, when we were organizing
rallies, I had my first encounter with the Rangers," José Angel
Gutiérrez recalls (interview, Albert Peña with José Angel
Gutiérrez, San Antonio, May 19, 1973). Gutiérrez, an honor
graduate of Crystal City High School, later founded La Raza
Unida, the political party that helped consolidate Chicano
political power in Texas. "After speaking at a rally I got a ride
home with friends, and they dropped me off at the house on the
corner of Edwards and Eighth Avenue. As my friends turned
the corner, the Rangers stopped them and blocked their car with
a car in front and one in the back. The officers had been
following us" (ibid.).

"The Rangers pulled my friends out of the car as I ran
across the street to help them. I got slapped immediately by
[Captain A. Y.] Allee. I didn't know the names of the other
Rangers. One car was full of deputies, though, and the other car
had Rangers in it. Allee was the one who slapped me. I fell
down and he kicked me once. That was all I was willing to take,
so I ran back to my house. The other boys also ran, but the
Rangers managed to get two boys into one car and took them to
jail, where they held them without filing charges. The Rangers
just scared them, telling them they weren't supposed to be at
these political rallies and that the rallies were Communist-
inspired. The Rangers told them it was no place for kids and that
we ought to stay home and get to school early" (ibid.).

"We had the voting booth episode next," remembers
García. "We had a trial run-around over absentee ballots. They
cut us from three polling places to one. Crystal City had never
had a secret ballot and the people had to vote right under the
eyes of the election judges. One of the oldest stories circulated
among Mexican Americans was about reprisals from one's boss
for voting, of being fired when he found out who you voted for.

And having a job was the most important thing to poor people" (interview, García).

According to García, Carlos Moore, the Teamsters' political expert from Dallas, was the perfect person to deal with the Anglo opposition at city hall. Moore drove a Cadillac into Crystal City, wore expensive suits, smoked big cigars, and always carried an election code book under his arm. "The people at city hall believed he was a lawyer," García recalls. "He told them either to set up a voting booth or he would file an injunction. Finally, we provided the booths as a gift from the Austin PASO Chapter—$42 for lumber and curtains, out of a timely $50 contribution. Then we got the run-around on the matter of having poll watchers. The official attitude was, 'We've never had any before, so that's that' " (ibid.).

The candidates and their supporters took the initiative to enforce the letter of the law in the election code. They took no chances on having fraudulent votes, mutilated ballots, or unreasonably disqualified voters. Moore pointed out the law on poll watchers to city manager James Dill and he agreed.

"The things they were denying us were so obvious on the face of it that the city attorney knew there was no use going to court," Fuentes recalls. "It was clearly written in black and white—candidates get poll watchers; voters have the right to a secret ballot; people who can't write get assistance; it's illegal to let nonresidents vote; it's illegal to let voters vote twice. All these were basic ground rules, but they had been ignored for years to make sure the elections came out the way the establishment wanted them. And the threats to go to court were not idle; they would have been carried out promptly.

"Charlie Albidress, a San Antonio attorney, did a great job training the poll watchers," Fuentes remembers. "We trained fifty or so and picked out the best twenty. Each of these people had a checklist of things to watch for. By the end of their training, these people knew more than the clerks about the do's and don'ts of voting" (interview, Fuentes).

Harrassment continued and intimidation escalated. "When the Rangers began to feel threatened, they conducted background searches on all of us," García remembers. "They found out that Carlos was a political expert from the Dallas Teamsters. They pursued one of the candidates, Mario Hernández, and put him in jail over a car repossession affair. As I went over to see about getting Mario out of jail, I ran across Allee in the Eagle Hotel. He told me things about myself that few people knew. For example, he told me that he knew my family had lived and worked on the King Ranch for three generations and were considered to be a good King Ranch family. He also knew that because of medical problems, I had gone to live with my grandfather and had adopted his last name. When I saw Allee that day, he came on just like a father. He said, 'You come from a good family. You don't belong here. The only thing that's going to happen to you is that you're going to get in trouble with people like Mario. Why don't you go home?' I had thought that I was invisible—that Allee didn't know anything about me. My driver's license certainly wouldn't have indicated my King Ranch heritage" (interview, García).

"Don't Leave Us Alone"

As the rallies began to attract more spectators and participants, the Rangers warmed up their counter-campaign. Confrontations resulted from disputes over the use of a sound truck and denial of the use of lights for the town square. "The city controlled the use of the Placita at night by removing the meter which provided the light," Henry Muñoz remembers. "We held one rally using the headlights of cars and trucks. By the time the election came, with the out-of-town press on hand, the city gave in and replaced the meter" (interview, Muñoz).

To draw attention to the rallies, Fuentes, García, and the candidates went through the neighborhoods with the sound truck announcing the rally featuring Jake Johnson and Johnny Alaniz, state representatives from San Antonio. "Allee stopped us," Fuentes recalls, "and told us it was against the law to use loudspeakers and that we would be jailed if we continued. Sheriff C. L. Sweeten and the chief of police showed up to back up Allee. I told them we were violating no city ordinance, and Carlos Moore said they could arrest us all and we would go to jail without resisting if they really wanted us to file individual suits for false arrest. Carlos said they had just told us they were going to arrest us for an act which no law prohibited.

"Jay Taylor, the city attorney, arrived and had Allee stay with us at the sound truck while he went to check through the city statutes to see if there was an offense we could be charged with. Although he reported there was no offense, Allee gave us all a stiff lecture, warning us that we would be held responsible for whatever trouble resulted. You would have thought there would be a law to protect us against violence, but we were harrassed anyway" (interview, Fuentes).

Representatives Johnson and Alaniz spoke at a rally nine days before the election and Alaniz later told Peña that people came up to him and Johnson afterwards saying, "*No nos dejen solos*"—"Don't leave us alone." They meant, after the election. And Johnson said in his speech, "I hope your people treat my gringo brothers better than the gringo has treated you" (Goodwyn, "Los Cinco Candidatos," p. 4).

Allee was the law, until the actual statutory law was read to him. García remembers that Allee would often pick up Mexican Americans, including himself and Muñoz, put them in his patrol car, sit there with the safety strap off the holster of his pistol, and give out orders. "It was always '*I don't want* any disturbance here. . . .' He would say, '*Your* people are doing this' or '*your* people are doing that' and recite a list of grievances. Allee lectured *us* while the property damage was being done to *our* cars and houses—windshields broken; nails put under tires; posters torn down; even Cornejo's house fired upon" (interview, García).

Calls for police assistance produced no relief. The law officers were not law enforcement officers for the Mexican Americans of Crystal City. García recalls that when a report of damage was made to the Ranger captain, "Allee would tell us we were getting just what we asked for. 'Politics was dangerous,' he said, 'and these things were the result.' He had no respect when he entered someone's house. He kept his hat on and walked in barking orders. Whomever Allee could identify as being in charge, he would try to dominate by giving orders—putting him down. He would tell him to go and do something, so he would know he was in control.

"Our strategy sessions were at the Veteran's Bar, next door to Juan's house," García notes. "The sessions were more like group therapy. We were trying to convince each other that they weren't going to hurt us and at the same time that we were going to win. One of the candidates told me, 'It's a good thing you're here, because that's what we needed all along—somebody who knows.' The fellow felt like our mutual knowledge protected him, and I wondered what protected me. I decided that armed with a law that I could get to work—I could protect myself. All the time I said we had support behind us in San Antonio. We have strong people up there, I said, who are going to come in and bail us out if we have trouble. The Rangers don't dare touch us for the eyes of the state are on this city.

"The third week after the filing deadline, the meetings became too large to be held indoors. When we moved outdoors, we could see Allee's car parked facing the meeting hall. He took over the city marshal's office, with [Rangers] Van Cleave, Russell, and A. Y. Allee, Jr. When Allee comes in he takes over the whole operation" (ibid.).

As Muñoz remembers the authority of the Rangers, the city marshal and county sheriff ceased to operate except as Allee's deputies. All law enforcement, including the requisite browbeating and intimidation was handled by Allee. "He assumed all law enforcement functions," Muñoz recalls. "In effect, Allee put the town under martial law. If there was a traffic violation, Allee wrote the ticket." An unofficial curfew was established and Mexican Americans walking alone at night were subject to verbal and physical abuse, as well as to arrest on a variety of false charges. A favorite target for punitive action was Chicano bars.

"Whenever Allee saw more than ten persons gathered in a bar, he would stop and shut it down," Muñoz says. "The Veteran's Bar was a favorite target, although other bars were also closed. They weren't closed because we were noisy or abusive, but because Allee felt that the Mexican Americans were stirring up trouble. He just shut the bars, and there was no argument. We would hold a rally and explain what had occurred and its significance. Two things happened each time they said 'no' to the law and we showed it to them. The Anglos' morale went down and the Chicanos' morale went up" (interview, Muñoz).

The rallies had the effect of keeping migrant Mexican Americans from leaving the city, even though the time for their joining the migrant stream and traveling northward had come two weeks before, and the night before election day, the largest rally of the campaign was held at the Placita with the crowd at 3,000 persons (interview, Fuentes). García gave the opening address in Spanish, saying "We're here tonight because deep in our hearts, we're all Mexicans and tomorrow we're going to go out and vote for our people" (Goodwyn, "Los Cinco Candidatos," p. 5). Fuentes continued in English, saying, "I want to tell our out-of-town guests that tonight we are seeing a people setting themselves free through the ballot box. . . . Do not be afraid, we will have people in the polling booth tomorrow to help you . . . the victory we win tomorrow is here tonight" (ibid.).

Each of the candidates then gave a speech, and Cornejo added, "I'm not scared of anything they might do. My life is for the people of Crystal City." García returned to say, "You have come to maturity, as we have in San Antonio. You have shown you are first class citizens willing to do everything you can for your country. Your *compadres* in San Antonio have come down here on their own time to help you. Now you must help others—in Sinton, Mathis, Baytown, Eagle Pass, and all the other towns where our people need help. There is discrimination in Texas and the only way we can stop it is through your vote." Fuentes closed the meeting with these words: "Go, in peace, to victory. Remember the words of the great Benito Juárez, 'Respect for others is peace' " (ibid.).

Election Day

On election day, the Rangers turned out in force. The *Texas Observer,* Texas's liberal bimonthly news organ, counted five Rangers, two state game wardens, two liquor control agents, Sheriff Sweeten, two deputies, the city marshal, and a deputy marshal—fourteen law enforcement officers in all (ibid.). Fuentes counted "fourteen or fifteen Rangers. There were some from Austin and Dallas and San Antonio that I recognized. The Rangers blocked off the street in front of city hall and the polling place" (interview, Fuentes).

On the side of the street next to the statue of Popeye there was no shade—the Mexican Americans stood there. Next to city hall, in the shade of a long row of commercial buildings, stood the Anglos. In the middle of the street stood the Rangers, the police, and the deputy sheriffs. Carlos Moore recalls that a complaint made to the Justice Department requesting federal marshals to protect the rights of the voters acted as a safety valve. Moore remembers, "although we never received a reply from the department, word passed that the marshals were indeed on the scene incognito. A large number of out-of-town onlookers were there that day and I think the sight of strangers in business suits cooled down the Rangers and kept them cooperative."

Larry Goodwyn of the *Texas Observer* staff interviewed City Attorney Jay Taylor during the balloting. "Certainly we're resentful of this union bunch coming in here and stirring up a bunch of rabble," Taylor told Goodwyn. "We never had any trouble before, or any discrimination" (Goodwyn, "Los Cinco Candidatos," p. 6). Taylor added that the pro-incumbent forces were worried, but that they were confident that they would win. "Our better Mexican element will not go along with the movement," he stated. "This is a good town. Shoot, I've seen some towns in South Texas where they won't even let Mexicans open a business downtown. We've never done that here. And we have a number of Mexican teachers in the schools" (ibid.). Taylor accounted for "an assistant football coach, the assistant band director and a Spanish teacher—all Latins" (ibid.). He missed counting the only other Chicano teacher on the high school staff of twenty-three—another Spanish teacher. Overall, in the Crystal City school system there were seventeen Mexican-American teachers of a total of 106. One incumbent councilman was quoted by Goodwyn as saying, "There's no discrimination, there's just too many of one race" (ibid.).

On election day the citizens committee received word that California Packing Company had doubled wages for that day. The company had, in effect, put employees on overtime from 5 a.m. to 10 p.m. Muñoz talked to the plant manager, who had several landowners in his office. "I told him," Muñoz recalls, "that the contract specified voting time off for employees. I said I represented the workers and if he didn't let the people off for two hours to vote, the company was going to be shut down." In the face of a quick strike, the manager kept his word to let the workers off between 10 a.m. and 12 noon. But the financial offer stood—double wages for employees not voting (interview, Muñoz).

"You know, for people who don't have much to eat, working for twice normal wages—providing they don't vote— presented a real dilemma," recalls Fuentes. "Yet I was proud of the people's choice. They said, 'No, we'll forego the extra pay. We've got to go vote.' They had listened, they had heard, they had learned, and now they believed." García also recalls that "without going home first the farmworkers got on trucks at four in the afternoon and came straight down to stand in line during the hottest part of the day" (interviews, Fuentes, García).

As the voting continued, it became apparent that a record number had turned out to vote. "It was incredible," Fuentes remembers. "We had used block-by-block canvassing, and it was hard work and time consuming. But it proved effective and the entire Mexican-American community became totally involved in the effort. Before the election, we put the registered voters on a card file, by precinct and by block. High school students learned how to mark paper ballots, and they in turn showed others. And I think the paper ballot is probably the meanest way to vote, because it's so easy to mess one up. We had sample ballots printed, and by election day, all of our people had practiced voting at least six times in their own homes. By the time they got to the ballot box, they weren't afraid or confused." For voters unable to read, Fuentes took a string, laid it on the paper ballot and knotted it by the names of the Chicano candidates (interview, Fuentes).

García remembers the routine of election day: "High school kids started showing up for doughnuts and coffee at six in the morning, picked up handfuls of cards, and by seven they had left to begin checking those who had voted. We had two lists going to check our progress—one at our nerve center in Juan's living room and the second one at the polls" (interview, García). If someone sent word that transportation was needed, a car or truck would be dispatched. As the afternoon wore on, runners were sent to registered voters' houses again to check on voting status. If the voters were ready to go down to city hall, a babysitter would be left to mind the children until the parents finished voting. "One young lady had to cook supper for the kids," Fuentes recalls. "People on crutches were even standing in line to vote. For many persons, this was the first time in their lives that they had actually voted" (interview, Fuentes).

The polls were scheduled to close at seven in the evening,

and shortly before closing time the line of voters began to dwindle. However, the crowd of spectators waiting for the results grew larger. A few minutes before seven, Fuentes talked to Allee in the middle of the street. "We wanted it clearly understood that anyone arriving prior to seven would be allowed to vote. It was the city's responsibility to provide sufficient voting places" (ibid.). Fuentes suggested that they use the normal practice to ensure that everyone in line by seven could vote. The clerk would go through the line, starting at the back, and collect all the poll taxes. Then he would have the people sit on the steps and come in one at a time.

"Sure enough, at seven o'clock there were only Chicanos in the line," Fuentes recalls, "and the clerk said it was too late to vote. It couldn't have been two minutes after I had talked to Allee. 'No use waiting,' one of the officials said, 'the polls are closing, it's too late.' " Fuentes started back toward Allee, but Allee had already had the law explained to him. For the moment he was beaten. He went into city hall and explained the law to the officials. "Of course he explained that we knew what the law was; *the election officials knew the law*," says Fuentes (ibid.). However, the poll taxes were collected and the people voted.

While the votes were being counted, García and Fuentes talked with the candidates about the campaign. "One of the things that struck me as being inaccurate at the very least in the newspaper accounts of the campaign," García remembers, "was the implication that there was a master plan directed by political bosses outside of Crystal City. The whole thing was so haphazard, even while they alleged it was masterminded by professional troublemakers. Some tactics weren't tactics at all; they were just emotions surfacing. There weren't more than four out-of-towners working in the campaign at any one time, other than when speakers were brought in from out of town for rallies" (interview, García).

Fuentes also remembers the charge of reverse racism made against the Mexican Americans. "I don't think at any time that anybody seriously said we wanted to wipe out the Anglos on the council. All we wanted was a majority. We had lit candles hoping for three seats, figuring we would do good to get two, and being satisfied with even one. But the furthest thing from our minds was wiping out all five Anglos" (interview, Fuentes).

Larry Goodwyn, the reporter for the *Texas Observer,* estimated the crowd waiting for the count as the evening advanced at "about a thousand people gathered on the square, some 750 on the plaza side, about 250 by the Ranger cars outside the drugstore." An 8:30 progress report, he said, showed the Anglos ahead for three of the five seats ("Los Cinco Candidatos," p. 7).

"The traffic was terrific," Muñoz recalls. The Rangers began to get irritated and started to tell individuals to go home. Allee approached Juan Cornejo and ordered, "Tell your people to go home." Cornejo replied that the people deserved to see the results. "It will be goddam midnight," replied Allee. "Goddam it, go home. It's going to be midnight" (interview, Muñoz).

Fuentes remembers that the Chicanos began to get restless and nervous about ten o'clock. "They thought the election was being stolen from them," Fuentes recalls. Five Mexican-American vote counters were inside city hall. At 10:30 one of the watchers ran out. "One in," he reported. Another watcher came out and said, "Two in." Then "Three and four." When the last counter reported, "Five in," according to Fuentes, pandemonium broke loose. "It could have been Times Square when World War II was over. I was standing beside the tall, slender deputy sheriff, who had been chewing tobacco. His mouth fell open and the tobacco hit the ground. All he could say was 'I'll be goddammed. They won 'em all' " (interview, Fuentes). The *Texas Observer* reported: "Allee appeared at the steps and was the first one in. He took one glance at the results, looked through the glass door at the marshals and gave a quick, time-honored gesture, an upsweep of his right fist. 'We got the shaft,' said a deputy" (Goodwyn, "Los Cinco Candidatos," p. 8).

The *Observer* recorded the official vote totals: Maldonado, 864; Cornejo, 818; Cárdenas, 799; Hernández, 799; Mendoza, 795; Ritchie, 754; Brennan, 717; Holsomback, 716; Bookout, 694; Galvan, 664; the two independents, 164 and 146 (ibid.). "Shock set in across the street," García recalls. "Out of 1,752 votes cast and a 97 percent turnout, *los cinco candidatos* had been elected" (interview, García).

The winners were hoisted up on shoulders, as were García and Fuentes. "Handshaking, honked horns, a couple of mexicano versions of the rebel yell and remarkably suddenly they fled to cars and dispersed under the long gazes of the Rangers," Goodwyn observed (Goodwyn, "Los Cinco Candidatos," p. 8).

The Ranger Captain and the New Council Members

García and Fuentes went to a trailer parked on Cornejo's lot, and Cornejo went to his home, which he shared with his mother and his married brothers. Goodwyn reported what happened next:

A patrol car pulled into the driveway. Allee got out and called for [Ray] Shafer [a San Antonio Teamster official], confronting him with hands on his hips, talking with the cigar in his teeth: "Shafer, this thing is getting out of hand. They are running all over the town honking their horns and shouting. Now we can't have this sort of thing. People are getting upset, Shafer. They figure you started this thing and they're mighty upset."

"What is it you want me to do?" asked Shafer.

"Where is your boy, Cornejo?"

"I guess he's over at his house."

"Well, let's go over there. He's got to control his people because this thing is getting out of hand." (Ibid.)

Goodwyn's report continues:

> Allee dominated the scene at Cornejo's house, a wooden
> structure no better and no worse than a thousand other mexicano
> homes there. A small group listened as Allee lectured Cornejo
> on his new responsibilities. Those who were drinking beer held
> the bottles with difficulty, like hot lead.
>
> "Cornejo, you're going to have to control your people. They
> must have respect," Allee said. A bystander, obviously tipsy,
> responded "Respect!" "Yes, respect." Some frantic movement
> and the bystander was escorted to the door. "That's right," said
> Captain Allee, "take the ——— out of here." (Ibid.)

Allee elbowed Cornejo as he stomped out; this was
witnessed by Muñoz, but discounted as an "accident" by
Cornejo.

> "We followed him to the Veteran's Bar next door," said
> García.". . . Allee went in there saying 'Your goddam people
> got to show some respect.' He told everyone to go home and he
> closed down the bar. As if the celebration was mob action on our
> part, as if we had no right or reason to celebrate. He spoke of
> 'those other people,' meaning the losers. 'How do you think they
> feel?' He threatened that 'they' might start an unnamed 'some-
> thing' that he couldn't protect us against." (Ibid.)

Reprisals after the election started at sunrise the next
morning. Maldonado, "the quiet one who campaigned the least
and led the ticket," as the *Texas Observer* described him, was
fired as assistant manager at the Economart. His employer
charged that he had campaigned on election day instead of
working. Maldonado said that he couldn't blame his employer,
because customers brought pressure on him and Maldonado had
refused to resign. However, there is no pay for a councilman's
job, and Maldonado had five children to support (ibid).

The next day, Cárdenas, who drove a truck for the Davis
Vacuum Truck Service, was told by his employer, Aubrey
David, that his salary had been cut from $77.44 a week to
$35.00. Mendoza, who had a Gulf service station, later lost the

dealership, and Hernández was squeezed for bad checks in his real estate and automobile transactions. Only Cornejo, who was protected by the union from economic reprisals, did not pay an economic price for winning his office.

Following adjournment of the first meeting of the new council, Cornejo remembers that Sheriff Sweeten shouldered him "like a common hoodlum" outside the chamber. "I didn't tell the newspapers," Cornejo said, "but there was a reporter from Laredo right there who saw it. He reported it" (ibid.).

At the next council meeting, a problem arose regarding the change of offices. Cornejo maintained decisions were to be made by the new council, not the old. Allee, who had the only key to the council chamber, attended the meetings and questioned the actions of the new council. Cornejo reminded Allee, "Wait a minute. I'm the mayor, and this is the city council. We decide this." Allee told him to "sit down and shut up." Cornejo replied, "I'm not going to sit down and shut up. That's why I was elected." Allee grabbed him by his lapel, slapped him across the face, and pushed him repeatedly into the wall, banging his head. "You little Mexican son-of-a-bitch, don't you talk to me like that. I'm the law around here," he ordered. "He told me that that was only an example. If I didn't keep my mouth shut to the papers it was going to get worse," recalls Cornejo (*San Antonio Express,* April 30, 1963, p. 12A).

That night the council members called Fuentes in San Antonio and made arrangements to charter an airplane. The pilot was to fly to Crystal City in the morning to take Cornejo out of town. "I didn't want Cornejo killed, and that's where it was headed," Fuentes recalls. "I chartered a plane the next morning to pick him up at the Crystal City airport, where they hid him overnight. Chris Dixie, a noted Houston labor attorney, agreed to file an injunction in federal district court to bar Allee from hurting Cornejo. We had to use what legal means we had to cool things down and protect the lives of the candidates" (interview, Fuentes).

The suit was filed on May 6, the day after Cornejo and

Councilman Antonio Cárdenas were quoted by the *San Antonio Express* as having been threatened by anonymous phone calls at 2:30 a.m. Dixie, as Cornejo's attorney, asked that Texas Ranger Captain A. Y. Allee be permanently restrained "from assaulting, intimidating, threatening or interfering, with Cornejo's constitutional rights." Besides the injunction, Dixie asked for $15,000 in actual and punitive damages. Judge Adrian Spears set the hearing for Del Rio the following October, six months away. "The case will be handled on the regular docket in the normal manner," Spears explained (*San Antonio Express,* May 8, 1963, p. 1).

Only City Manager James Dill, County Commissioner Tom Allee, the Ranger captain's cousin, and Sheriff Sweeten had witnessed the assault. Dill and Sweeten denied Cornejo's account, Dill saying, "the captain didn't lay a hand on him" (*San Antonio Express,* May 7, 1963). Tom Allee said that the captain did tell "Cornejo in words he could understand" that he didn't appreciate Cornejo's words to the newspapers. At first Allee told the *Express,* "He's a liar." But he told Martin García, "You don't think I beat him up? I told the little son-of-a-bitch to quit poppin' off to the papers. I took him by the collar and shook him up a little bit." Then later Allee told Sam Kindrick of the *Express,* "Hell, I didn't whip the mayor, it's just politics and I guess somebody put him up to accusing me of roughing him up." "Sure we get a little rough sometimes," the captain continued, "but if I'd banged Cornejo's head against the wall you wouldn't have seen him flying off to the papers right afterwards. He wouldn't have been able to" ("Shock Waves from Popeye Land," *Texas Observer,* May 16, 1963, p. 1).

The implied prediction for future violence was clear. Telegrams were sent to Governor John Connally, Attorney General Waggoner Carr, Senator Ralph Yarborough, and United States Attorney General Robert F. Kennedy, signed by Cornejo, the other members of the city council, and prominent San Antonio political figures. The telegrams to Governor Connally and Attorney General Carr asked for a state investigation into civil rights violations in Crystal City. "We are in a state of fear and intimidation," Cornejo's telegram read. "We need help" (*San Antonio News,* May 9, 1963, p. 1).

Governor Connally replied: "The Texas Rangers were sent to Crystal City for the sole purpose of maintaining law and order and to prevent violence. Apparently their efforts have been successful to date and they will remain as long as the situation warrants. Every effort will be made to insure that the elected officials may perform their duties. I urge your cooperation" (ibid.).

Cornejo and other citizens immediately objected to Connally's taking the Rangers' side before investigating the charges. Tomás M. Rodríguez sent the governor a telegram saying that he "and a substantial group of our citizens of Latin extraction are greatly surprised and concerned" about Connally's endorsement of Allee's attitude and activities (ibid.). Rodríguez's message understated the community's fear.

Attorney General Carr, technically the people's lawyer, turned Cornejo's charges over to the director of the Department of Public Safety, Homer Garrison, who also serves as head of the Texas Rangers. Carr stated, "I have great confidence in Colonel Garrison. There seems to be great division among people in the area over this" (*San Antonio Express,* April 30, 1963, p. 1). Not only did Carr fail to investigate the so-called "division," he turned the citizens' plea for protection from the Rangers over to a Ranger.

Before he investigated the allegations, Garrison reached his conclusions and announced them. "No complaints have been made to me," he said, ignoring Cornejo's complaint. "The only thing we are doing is keeping the peace. I know the peace has been kept" (ibid.).

Tensions were again raised when a Greek-American deputy sheriff from San Antonio, Eugene Foitios, was arrested and charged with illegally carrying a pistol. Foitios told the Rangers he was in Crystal City to work for San Antonio police sergeant Bob Cruz, who had been mentioned as possible city marshal by the council. Allee telephoned Bexar County Constable Joe Ferro, who relieved Foitios of his authority. "He didn't have any business carrying a gun down there," Ferro said. "I cancelled his commission. Captain Allee is the law down there" (ibid).

When Senator Ralph Yarborough learned that Cornejo's charges had been denied by Allee, the senator upheld the councilmen he had publicly congratulated after their election. In Dallas he denounced "men wearing pistols, not a part of city government but breathing down the necks of duly elected men as they exercise the functions of their offices." Such men, Yarborough continued, "are a relic of a primitive age in Texas which should have passed away with the frontier," and added: "This is the most flagrant and extraordinary usurpation of power I have heard of since the oil boom days in Borger and before that in Reconstruction" ("Shock Waves from Popeye Land," p. 1).

Petition to Recall

Meanwhile city employees resigned rather than work for the new council. A. J. Hale, the city utility superintendent, turned in his keys. City Manager Dill resigned, referring to Section 20 of the city charter as his reason for his resignation. Section 20 forbids the council from interfering with appointments and dismissals, responsibility for which lies solely with the city manager (*San Antonio Light,* May 1, 1963, p. 1).

Dill had little else to say during the city council session, while Mario Hernández spoke of the rapid change and brought out the arguments that he was hearing from Anglos. Dill left immediately after the vote to accept his resignation, which carried 3–1. But a *San Antonio Express* reporter talked with him outside the chambers and reported: "The manager says he hopes charges are filed against Allee. 'We're ready for them if they do,' he said. 'We'll tear this administration all to pieces' " *(San Antonio Express,* April 30, 1963, p. 1).

Hernández made statements to the press echoing the Anglo rationale for the use of the Rangers. The *Express* also quoted Hernández on "outsiders," who charged that it was Fuentes's decision to fire the city manager and that Ray Shafer, San Antonio Teamster official, made the decision to elect Cornejo mayor. "I'll take help from anyone," he said, "but I'm a city councilman now. I'll take advice from anyone, too, but I won't have people from San Antonio telling me how to run my town" *(San Antonio Express,* May 6, 1963, p. 1).

The same *Express* article indicated that Cornejo and the other councilmen viewed Hernández's statements with alarm. Cárdenas was quoted at the time as saying, "The Rangers have gotten to him. They have him under their thumb. They must have something on him" (ibid.). Mendoza was skeptical of the depth of Hernández's dissent. "He doesn't have anything against PASO and the Teamsters. If not for them," Mendoza said, "we would never have been elected" (ibid.).

Hernández finally admitted to Fuentes that he had indeed been pressured. "He admitted that if he had not spoken out in a way to disrupt the unity of the councilmen," recalls Fuentes, "that Jackson, the county attorney, was going to carry through on his threat to prosecute him for passing bad checks. If he had only told us of the pressure before, but it was the usual tactic—blackmailing and coercing through the selective use of the law" (ibid.).

The former city administration, the county administration, businessmen, and the Rangers lined up in a solid block against the new councilmen. Members of the Zavala County Commissioner's Court passed a resolution praising Texas Ranger Captain Allee, his Rangers, Sheriff C. L. Sweeten, his deputies, and county attorney G. Curtis Jackson "for their efforts without which chaos probably would have resulted" (ibid.). Holding back support of the resolution was Harry

Reynolds of precinct four, who refused to take sides. Voting in favor of the resolution were County Judge John L. Pegues and Commissioners W. B. Brown, Warren Wagner, and Tom Allee.

The ousted council members used two other harrassing tactics to break the spirit of the councilmen. County attorney Jackson proposed to challenge the qualifications of two of the councilmen on the basis of property ownership. Although no one was sure of the charter provisions, in February Cornejo had transferred his house into his name from his mother's name. In his family the mother held title to the property from the late father, and all money earned by members of the family went into a common fund. The challenge grew into a recall petition spearheaded and publicly crusaded for by Commissioner Tom Allee and circulated with the backing of the remaining Anglo officeholders. The petition proposed to amend the city charter and to force a new election in October, with all the councilmen standing for reelection. According to the *San Antonio Express-News*, Allee said his purpose was to get the present councilmen out of office and start from scratch. "Under the terms of the city charter," Allee explained, "only 10 percent of the registered voters are needed to call an election. We have at least 400 signatures, about 25 percent of the voters. The city council probably will object, but they will have to call an election and I think they will be unseated" (June 18, 1963, p. 1).

Mayor Cornejo recognized the petition as harrassment and was determined to meet it head on. He said the council would not contest the petitions, "but just beat them again. If they want another election," he said, "they'll get it. If they haven't learned their lesson yet, we'll just have to teach them again." The mayor further stated that plans were being laid for a fall election "if the petitions lived up to the charter." "We've already started making contact with families up north," he said, referring to migrant workers. "When the time comes to vote each one will be sent an absentee ballot" (ibid.).

Major coverage was given to the recall petition by the state's conservative press. Although notable by its absence at the scene during the campaign, the conservative press joined the governor, the attorney general, the head of the State Department of Public Safety, and the county court in voicing confidence in the Texas Rangers. On May 7, the *Dallas Morning News* headlined a story by conservative columnist Jimmy Banks entitled "Dealt a Poor Hand, Teamsters Take All." Banks contended that the Teamsters had dealt themselves a "pitiful" hand, five "poorly educated Latin American candidates and then raked in all the chips. Shafer runs the only game in Crystal City," Banks wrote (May 7, 1963, p. 1). According to Banks's information, the town's credit rating was "none" and retail sales had dropped drastically. "It was largely this vast horde of Latin Americans, most of whom had never voted before, that the Teamsters—reinforced by PASO—herded to the polls to sweep all five places on the city council," Banks stated (ibid.).

Shafer was interviewed by James McCrory of the *San Antonio Express* staff. "Ray Shafer, business agent for the San Antonio Teamsters, named by one of the Crystal City councilmen as one of the men calling the shots in Crystal City, said he is definitely not giving orders or advice to Crystal City officials on how to run their city," McCrory reported. "He said Cornejo is in close touch with him daily on Teamsters Union business, 'but we haven't discussed appointments or city operations. Mr. Cornejo hasn't asked me what he should do' said Shafer. 'I gave them what assistance I could during the election, but it stopped right there. I think they have a good city manager and can run their own city' " (May 6, 1963, p. 1).

Hart Stilwell, writing in the *Texas Observer*, blamed the victim, just as Banks had in the *Dallas Morning News*. Stilwell ignored the pervasive discrimination in the electoral system, which made it appear that Mexican Americans were subverting election ground rules. He carefully distinguished between winning a majority and shutting out the minority—without taking note of the particular conditions of Crystal City. "A lot of people are making a lot of noise because five people with Spanish names won control," Stilwell wrote. "There are more Chicanos than gringos in Crystal City, why not make it an exclusive Chicano government and shut out the gringo? 'Why not?'

"When Chicanos win a majority on a governing body where they constitute a population majority, nothing but justice is being served. When they decide, because they can, to shut out the racial minority completely, then they are doing exactly what the segregationists have been doing for so many years" ("Another Comment," *Texas Observer*, May 16, 1963, p. 4).

Stilwell generalized a widely used double standard—discrimination against Mexican Americans is unfortunate, but sudden reversals going against Anglos are criminally discriminatory. He went on to say, "Whereas if PASO and the Teamsters had been content with a mere majority of three and not completely shut out Anglos, race hatred and discrimination would not have built up. It is possible to keep a racial majority repressed if that racial majority owns little of the town's wealth. But never in history has a group economically dominant been shut permanently from the operation of a city or state. There is going to be a brutal tightening down on the Mexican American in every town in South Texas," Stilwell predicted, "because of what PASO and the Teamsters so arrogantly pulled off" (ibid.).

"Fuentes, García and the councilmen agreed that there was no inherent reason why Anglos should not be elected by Chicanos. Fuentes said the one way he cannot stop being racial lies in the fact that he is a Mexican and cannot choose whether he will be discriminated against because he is a Mexican." Stilwell concluded, "I think a bit of trickery—and that's what it was to a large extent—pulled off by PASO and the union is going to backfire until both organizations wish they had never heard of Crystal City" (ibid.).

The intimidating actions of the Anglo citizens struck fear

in the council members and the Mexican-American citizens of Crystal City. "The Anglo community—being ranch types and not used to having their authority and their dominance threatened—was (and is) violence prone. After the election, with the press all around, I was not so scared of the Rangers as of some crazy Anglo with a gun in his hand" (interview, García). He recounted one incident: "Some kids pulled a gun on me outside a restaurant. I was outside waiting, and there were three kids in one of those zoomed-up cars. One was pointing a gun at me and said, 'Hey you Mexican, you better get out of town!' I got brave for a second and walked up in front of him and told him something to the effect that, 'if you point that gun at me, you'd better use it.' They just must have been playing games, as they took off. I called a deputy sheriff to investigate, but nothing was done about it. I don't know how many times that kind of thing was done in the community, but I bet it occurred to a lot of people. Emotions were very high" (ibid.).

The *San Antonio Express* carried an Associated Press report of new economic reprisals. According to the AP report, Colonel D. Harold Byrd, one of the area's largest producers and shippers, and the man who had erected the statue of Popeye in the town square, was moving his headquarters and processing facilities from Crystal City to the nearby town of La Pryor. The report stated, "Highly critical of Teamster involvement, Byrd termed the union's activity 'a terrible cancer that is spreading' " *(San Antonio Express,* May 5, 1963, p. 1).

According to Byrd's version, law and order seemed to be the exclusive province of Anglo city administrators. Byrd estimated the payroll loss to Crystal City to be $50,000 a month, an estimate which would seem to bankrupt him by $100,000 in wages alone each year. Cornejo revealed that Byrd paid starvation wages and was the last resort for job hunters in the area. Byrd also revealed his personal political bias in the Associated Press story by describing Senator Ralph Yarborough's support of Cornejo and other city officials as "way out in left field. Instead of the Rangers being troublemakers, it is these Teamster intruders who came into this peaceful community and agitated the people who are looked on scornfully by most of the good Mexican citizens of Crystal City" (ibid.).

In response to questions from a *Wall Street Journal* staff reporter, Albert Fuentes called Byrd's threat an overblown tactic. Recalling the *Journal* reporter's question, Fuentes said: "The fellow came down and asked me, 'Sure you won the city election but they control the money. What are you going to do when the money people take their business out of town?' He mentioned Byrd's name, so we took a drive out to see the 5,000 acres. I said, 'Let me tell you something. This area has a 360-day growing season. When Byrd figures out how to move his 5,000 acres and its growing season out of this area, then I'll become concerned. In the meantime he's got 5,000 acres only the Lord can move, loaded with vegetables that must be picked, and only the Chicanos will pick them. He's not going anywhere' " (interview, Fuentes).

A Failure and a Success

Although the recall petition was never officially filed, the Anglo community succeeded in splitting the unity and effectiveness of the council. Lacking political sophistication in coping with determined opposition, the council gradually lost momentum in bringing about change in Crystal City and succeeded in casting serious doubts in both Anglo and Mexican-American citizens as to the council's ability to administer city responsibilities. As time went on, the local PASO chapter factionalized and lost its image as a viable organizing committee, and the Teamsters backed away from both the council and PASO as a result of statewide criticism. As a result of Anglo harrassment, when the 1965 elections came around the organizing effort to which many Crystal City residents had devoted so much time had split and lost its momentum. Not all the candidates ran for reelection, and the Anglos regained control of the city council.

However, in 1970, under the leadership of José Angel Gutiérrez, politically educated Chicanos successfully won a majority of seats on both the Crystal City school board and the city council, which they have retained to this time. Under their leadership, both the city and the school system entered a new period of progressive government, responsive to the local community rather than to an elite few.

Education and the Rangers

The problem of Anglo oppression in Crystal City did not end in 1965. In 1968, Chicanos, realizing the power of a concerted effort, turned their attention to the school system. When public schools were established in Crystal City, only an elementary school had to be segregated for the Chicanos. Mexican Americans were expected to drop out before high school, and the rationale became a self-fulfilling prophecy.

In earlier years, a graduating class typically consisted of twenty-five or thirty Anglos and one or two Mexican Americans. Throughout the 1960s, the percentage of Mexican-American graduates grew. However, student organizations and student activities remained basically Anglo—partly because the Anglo faculty and administration arranged it that way. The teachers who selected cheerleaders always seemed to settle on one Mexican American and three Anglos (Shockley, 1974, p. 116 and passim).

In Crystal City, the predominance of Anglo cheerleaders became a symbol of dominance to Anglos and a symbol of oppression to Chicano students. In 1969, after the selection of the cheerleaders, Chicano students began a protest that eventually led to Crystal City's having all Chicano cheerleaders, a Chicano majority on the school board, a Chicano superintendent, and many more Chicano teachers.

In the 1969 spring semester there were 2,540 Chicano students—86 percent of the total enrollment—in the Crystal City system, compared to 376 Anglos and 12 blacks (Census Bureau Report, 1970). Two student leaders, Severita Lara and Armando Trevino, presented a petition to Principal John B. Lair complaining about the disproportionate number of Anglo cheerleaders. Lair rejected the complaint. The petition then was sent to Superintendent John Billings, who said he would see to it that two more cheerleaders would be added so that there would be a three-to-three split.

The alumni association always elected the homecoming queen. Eligibility for homecoming queen required that at least one parent be a graduate of Crystal City High School and this eligibility almost automatically eliminated Chicano girls from consideration. The high school football team—dominated by Anglos—elected its own football sweetheart; however, the baseball team—which always had a Chicano majority—was told to elect two sweethearts, an Anglo and a Mexican American. Students presented a list of grievances to the school board and its response was the passage of a policy statement transferring the favorite's selection to the student body, establishing judges from outside the school district to select majorettes and cheerleaders, and establishing faculty prerogatives over most representative honors.

To protest the ex-students association's domination of homecoming queen, Severita Lara published a leaflet denouncing the procedure. When she distributed it on campus, she was promptly suspended for three days. However, through the efforts of the Mexican American Legal Defense Fund (MALDEF), she was allowed back into school after two days of her suspension.

At the school board meeting on November 10, the Chicano students presented their second list of grievances.

After permitting speeches and comments, the school board took the list under advisement. On December 8, most of the Chicano high school students attended the board meeting to see what answer the board had prepared for their complaints. With three members absent, a motion was passed by a three-to-one vote declaring that after a careful study of the situation no instances of discrimination were found and since many of these matters were administrative the board would take no action.

The next day a walkout of junior high school and high school students began. Seven hundred persons marched in support of the striking students the next day. Ciudadanos Unidos, a parent's organization, met on December 12 and voted to take their children out of the school system. By the second week of the boycott, 1,500 children were refusing to attend school.

Following the traditional line of attack, the Anglos blamed outside agitators for the protest. This time the blame was placed on José Angel Gutiérrez. Gutiérrez had all the attributes of an outside agitator—he was both educated and articulate. However, the native Anglos had forgotten that he had been born in Crystal City and had been president of the 1962 senior class at Crystal City High School. The son of a doctor, Gutiérrez had been the kind of student Anglos like to point to as an example of how a bright and ambitious Mexican American could get ahead. After founding the Mexican American Youth Organization (MAYO) and earning his master's degree in government, Gutiérrez returned to Crystal City to help with the boycott.

Working with the same techniques he had used to found MAYO, he strived to unite the Crystal City Chicanos into an effective political action group. What evolved was La Raza Unida, a new Chicano-based political group that eventually became a focal point for Chicano political action in Texas and in other parts of the Southwest.

By the time of the 1969 school walkout in Crystal City, many of the Mexican Americans had become veterans of confrontations. The leaders knew the tactics the Rangers used and were prepared to meet them with action. Mass meetings were held in the town plaza. Reluctant parents were drawn in by the participation of their children. Severita Lara recalls many parents' attitudes: "At first most of the parents were scared and couldn't see the use. But we told them the homecoming queen was just an issue, that there were other things that really mattered. Teachers insulted us by calling us names, the school books were Anglo oriented, and the Chicanos received no academic counseling" (interview, Albert Peña with Severita Lara, San Antonio, July 10, 1973).

The Rangers also attended the open-air meetings. "The police always showed up, and Allee was very much in appearance. They took notes and followed people," Lara recalls. She also alleged that a pickup truck tried to run over her (ibid.).

Meeting the educational needs of the striking students was a decided problem and one the community could not meet alone. Texans for the Educational Advancement of Mexican Americans (TEAM) volunteered to teach the boycotting students during the walkout. Classes were held wherever possible—in city parks, at a Chicano movie house, at a Chicano dance hall, at a funeral home, and in private homes.

During the Christmas holidays, the three Chicano student teachers, Armando Trevino, Severita Lara, and Diana Serna flew to Washington, D.C., at Senator Ralph Yarborough's expense to talk with Department of Health, Education, and Welfare (HEW) officials, as well as with Senators Edward Kennedy and Yarborough. Through Justice Department efforts, the school board agreed to meet with five parents, five students, and three observers. After negotiating for four days, the school board and the striking students reached agreement. The trustees capitulated to all the students' demands except freedom of the press, speech, and dress. Students, nevertheless, agreed to forgo those guarantees for the moment. After nearly a month of picketing, the striking students entered classes again on the morning of January 6.

A Victory for La Raza Unida

As an organizing tool for Gutiérrez, the boycott became a movement. Although the issue of the boycott originally evolved over the selection of the high school's cheerleaders, it eventually led to the organization of community discussion groups, registration of voters, and acquisition of control over the school board and the council. In the spring of 1970, with the boycott organization still intact to register voters, Gutiérrez and two other Chicano candidates ran for the school board as candidates of the La Raza Unida Party. When the La Raza candidates won, they joined with a Mexican American already on the board to form a four-to-three majority. The board's first official act was to elect José Angel Gutiérrez its president. The school board meetings, formerly held in a conference room, had to be moved to the high school cafeteria and finally to the auditorium to accommodate the citizens who wanted to ask questions or state opinions (interview, Gutiérrez).

The school boycott accomplished three ancillary goals: it established the consumer power of the Chicanos who boycotted businesses not in sympathy with the boycott; it provided issues to raise the community's political awareness; and it exposed the depth of Anglo racism and how the balance of power in the community could be changed. Chicanos first saw the vulnerability of the school, in a business sense, for it lost state per capita funds when its students refused to go to school. Anglo businesses were also boycotted to persuade businessmen to reason with the school board. Chicanos saw that Chicano money kept Anglos in positions of power in Crystal City and that Anglos could be made to accept social change through public economic sanctions.

However, the use of these sophisticated political techniques by Chicanos gained them the ire of both law enforcement officials and businessmen in the community. County deputies arrested two youngsters in front of the school for abusive language, and storekeeper J. L. Spears fired two high school students for participating in the walkout. While picketing the store to protest Spears's actions, Gutiérrez was stopped by three Rangers and Sheriff Sweeten. "I was informed that if I continued explaining the purpose of the picketing to onlookers, the Rangers would arrest me for inciting a riot" Gutiérrez recalls (interview, Gutiérrez).

Even though an adjacent store was closed, since it was Saturday, the Rangers arrested Severita Lara and her sister Linda for obstructing its entrance. Del Rio attorney Mike González met the Rangers at the jail and argued for the girls' release. The Rangers returned and gave Gutiérrez twenty minutes to disperse the growing crowd of Chicanos or face a mass arrest. "It was twenty minutes to seven, the store's closing time," Gutiérrez remembers. "At fifteen minutes before the hour, the Rangers came up to tell me there were only fifteen minutes left—then ten minutes—then five minutes. They would have no choice, they said, but to place everyone under arrest. Then it was seven o'clock and the store closed" (ibid.).

Gutiérrez strolled over and told the Rangers the crowd was now leaving since the store was closed. The Rangers backed down. "It was the first time I had seen Rangers and the county police afraid of handling a public situation," Gutiérrez says. He also recalls: "The Rangers stood around me with unlit cigars in their mouths, telling me that they were not going to put up with this the next day. I lit a cigarette, lit their cigars, and told them I didn't believe anything they said. If they were going to do anything, I told them, they were going to do it today and threats wouldn't prevent La Raza from taking action. I told them we wished they would stop bothering us. There were a lot of people standing around, and I realized they just didn't have the guts to carry out any threats. For the first time—perhaps in the century—they turned and walked away" (ibid.).

John Connally's
Strikebreakers

THE TEXAS RANGERS, under the leadership of Captain Allee, had had a strong taste of Mexican-American activism in politics and education in Crystal City, and it left a bitter taste in their mouths. The next confrontation between the two occurred on the battlefield of economics in another town not far away.

Rio Grande City in Starr County in Texas's Lower Rio Grande valley is an area that has always been marked by revolution. Indian raids, filibustering activities, and punitive expeditions were all part of the early history of the area. Between the Mexican-American War and the Civil War, Rio Grande City served as an outpost for revolutionary activities that extended over the border into Mexico. As one account, published by the Rio Grande City Chamber of Commerce, states

> Along the Border were gathered many adventurers lately discharged from the army that had invaded Mexico and others that had simply "Gone to Texas." All had a profound lack of interest in wrestling a plow or any sweat-producing effort. They were a picturesque, irresponsible crew ready for a filibustering expedition, cattle rustling in Mexico or a bit of smuggling. The other side of the Rio Grande furnished rustlers and raiders also. ("A Short History of Rio Grande City," n.d., p. 1)

Rio Grande City was a fitting place for the most publicized clash between Mexican-American farmworkers and the Texas Rangers, a clash that led to an investigation by members of

131

Congress and to court cases that focused on the civil rights of Mexican-American farmworkers in the Rio Grande valley.

To understand the struggle between the farmworkers and the Texas Rangers that marked the latter part of the 1960s as a period of great labor unrest in Texas, it is necessary to look first at the socio-economic picture of South Texas. The Rio Grande valley of Texas, one of the principal farm areas of the nation, has a population sharply divided into a series of socio-economic levels. At the very top are the owners and managers of farming interests who profit from the products grown in the fertile valley. At the bottom are the farmworkers, the poor, most of whom are Mexican American. Many workers have recently come from Mexico, while others are native Americans unable to break the poverty cycle. In 1966 union organizers found that farmworkers in the Rio Grande valley went to work in the fields for as little as twenty-five cents an hour.

It was in this setting that activist Eugene Nelson was able to organize the workers into the new Independent Workers Association (IWA) and to begin a strike against eight major growers on June 1, 1966. On June 8 the IWA voted to affiliate with the National Farm Workers Association (NFWA) of César Chávez. (Nelson was one of Chávez's organizers during the Delano grapepickers strike.) By striking, the union sought to organize the valley farmworkers by representing them on labor questions and to raise the hourly wage for agricultural labor to $1.25 an hour.

Also on June 8, a Starr County deputy sheriff arrested Nelson at the Roma, Texas International Bridge. Nelson was near the bridge attempting to persuade laborers from Mexico to support the strike by refusing to work on farms in the United States. He was taken to the courthouse in Rio Grande City where he was held for about four hours without charges being filed against him. During the time Nelson was held, he was questioned by the Starr County attorney, who asked him about his activities regarding the strike. The attorney intimidated Nelson by telling him, falsely, that he was under investigation by the FBI in regard to an alleged threat to blow up the courthouse and destroy the buses being used by local farms to transport Mexican laborers to work (*Medrano* v. *Allee* 347 F. Supp. 605 [1972] p. 612).

"Viva La Huelga!"

In an effort to call attention to the plight of the farmworker, a march was organized for July 4, 1966, which included approximately one hundred Rio Grande City agricultural workers and two thousand supporters. The event was originally planned as a four- or five-day march through the valley, but a group of the marchers turned north, with the intention of presenting to Governor John Connally their demands that Texas's agricultural workers be included under the state's $1.25-per-hour minimum wage law. The march ended with a massive rally on the grounds of the state capitol at Austin.

The march received a good deal of publicity and favorable reaction from liberal labor groups and both moral and financial support from a variety of religious groups. Some individual religious representatives made personal sacrifices. One Church of Christ minister from McAllen was removed from his post by elders of his church for refusing to abandon the march. Support from the Catholic Church, many of whose members were agricultural workers in the state, included money, food, and clothing, as well as the prayers and moral support of the church ("Valley Bishop to Offer Mass for 'Huelgistas' in San Juan," *Alamo Messenger*, July 9, 1966, p. 1).

The striking marchers were led by Father Anthony González, OMI, and by the Reverend James L. Novarro, a Baptist minister. Catholic priests offered mass for the "huelgistas" as they passed through their respective towns, and on several occasions the church donated food, clothing, and money to the marchers (ibid.; also, " 'Huelga' Comes to S.A.," *Alamo Messenger*, August 26, 1966, p. 1).

En route to Austin, the marchers stopped at Governor Connally's hometown of Floresville and extended to the governor and his brother an invitation to greet them. However, neither of the men responded to the invitation. While they were in Floresville, the marchers learned that the executive council of the AFL–CIO had granted them an organizing charter. Eugene Nelson, coordinator of the march, voiced his optimism that the news of the charter would persuade the governor to meet the marchers at the capitol on Labor Day.

Senator Ralph Yarborough briefly joined the marchers in San Antonio. In his sermon to the marchers, the Most Reverend Robert E. Lucey, Archbishop of San Antonio, stated that "a wage of a dollar and a quarter an hour is a ghastly recompense for exhausting labor under the burning sun of Texas." He urged Texans of Mexican descent to "stand up and defend themselves against discrimination and oppression" (Crawford and Keever, 1973, p. 230).

Nelson's optimism that Connally would meet with the marchers proved to be well-founded—but the governor met them not in Austin, not on Labor Day, and not for the reasons Nelson had hoped. On August 31, Governor Connally, Lieutenant Governor Ben Barnes, and Attorney General Waggoner Carr, a candidate for the U.S. Senate, decided to drive to New Braunfels to intercept the marchers on their way to Austin. The marchers were informed of Connally's imminent arrival by reporters who raced ahead of the governor's limousine. The leaders of the march were hopeful that this was meant to be an extraordinary gesture of goodwill on the part of the governor. Connally and his entourage were greeted warmly. The governor, however, informed march leaders González and Novarro that neither he nor any other top state officials would meet them when they arrived in Austin, adding that even if he were in Austin on Labor Day, "I do not think I would have met you simply because my door is open; it has been open since this march began on July 4" (ibid., p. 232).

The arrival of Eugene Nelson and Hank S. Brown, Texas

AFL–CIO president, caused the meeting between the governor and the strikers to become even more strained. Nelson asked Connally to take the leadership in calling a special session of the legislature to enact a minimum wage law. Connally replied: "I tell you categorically that I will not call a special session for this purpose because I don't think the urgency of it is of such a character that it has a compelling nature to it, so the answer to that is no" (ibid.). As to whether or not he would meet the marchers at the capitol he told the men, "I do not feel that as governor of this state I should lend the dignity, the prestige, of an office to dramatize a particular march, and so I would not have been with you even if I had not had a previous commitment. I want to make that clear" (ibid.). As he had promised, Connally was not present on Labor Day when the hundred Rio Grande valley farmworkers and their by now ten thousand supporters walked the final miles to the state capitol building in Austin.

Senator Ralph Yarborough addressed the marchers, telling them that a state minimum wage law was necessary in order that "you can buy food so there will be something in the stomachs of your hungry children so they can go to school" ("Huelgistas Push Strike," *Alamo Messenger,* September 9, 1966, p. 14). Senator Robert Kennedy sent a telegram commending the marchers, and César Chávez and Texas labor leaders Henry Muñoz and Hank S. Brown also attended the capitol rally. Two vigils were left at the capitol following the rally, and Father Anthony González said that those keeping the vigil "would ask God to soften the heart of our governor and those around him, because I am sure that the governor—and I still believe this—is the friend of the people. He is the governor in whom the Latin believes" (ibid.).

Connally refused to call a special session to settle the question of the farmworkers' minimum wage, and when the legislature convened again in 1967, the $1.25 minimum wage was rejected. The flags and banners of the valley farmworkers, flown at the capitol since the march began were finally taken down.

"A Respectful Place"

The governor's refusal to support the minimum wage was a disappointment, but it did not dampen the farmworkers' will to continue the protest during the fall of 1966. About twenty-five union members and sympathizers were picketing along U.S. Highway 83 next to Rancho Grande Farms on October 12, urging field hands to join the strike. At the request of farm officials, Starr County deputies arrived and ordered the pickets to disperse, which they did. One of the union leaders, William Chandler, who engaged a deputy in conversation, questioning the validity of the order, was arrested for violation of Article 474 of the Texas Penal Code, involving breech of the peace. He was taken to the courthouse and placed under $500 bond even though it was a charge that could only carry a maximum punishment of a $200 fine (*Medrano* v. *Allee,* pp. 612–613).

Twelve days after Chandler's arrest, another incident occurred. Domingo Arredondo, president of the union in Starr County, and several union members found themselves under arrest in the courthouse. While in a hall, Arredondo shouted "Viva la Huelga" in support of the strike. A deputy sheriff then struck Arredondo in the face, pushed him backwards, and put a cocked pistol against his forehead, ordering him not to repeat those words in that building because the courthouse was a "respectful place" (ibid.).

Enter the Rangers

The Texas Rangers had been on something resembling "stand-by alert" ever since the strike began. Whenever the fear of potential Mexican-American gains flared up, or when it was recognized that a situation might be useful in discrediting the strikers, the Texas Rangers were activated. During the thirteen months of the strike, a climate of accusation and counter-accusation prevailed.

Perhaps the most serious of these accusations against the strikers came in November 1966, when a fire at a railroad trestle was blamed on the strikers, and the Missouri Pacific Railroad and Starr County officials requested, and received, the help of the Texas Rangers. It was never proved that the strikers or their supporters had been responsible for the fire, and it would seem that the Rangers were called in because they represented a police force that could operate in various counties, not in Starr County alone.

Mexican Americans in Texas felt, however, that the Rangers were brought in because of their experience in strike-breaking, their experience with the enforcement of Texas's tough anti-union laws, and their experience with doing the politically distasteful work of arresting strikers—work especially distasteful and awkward to political officials very much aware of the rising political activism of the Mexican Americans of South Texas. The Raza Unida movement had not yet completely materialized, but the earlier victory in local elections by Mexican Americans in Crystal City was still fresh in the minds of local officials and workers alike.

The Rangers, as confirmed in subsequent court testimony, acted in the capacity of strikebreakers, not law enforcement officers—they used the tools of their position as lawmen to stop the strikers. On November 9 the Rangers arrested several strikers, including Reynaldo De La Cruz. Court evidence in the case of *Medrano* v. *Allee* brought out the fact that two Rangers advised De La Cruz that he could work for La Casita Farms for $1.25 an hour, the wage demanded by the union, and that later the workers could organize a more peaceful union. De La Cruz was further advised that the Rangers were there to break the strike and would not leave until they had done so (ibid., p. 613).

On November 28, the union held a rally on the grounds of the Starr County courthouse, with various banners and flags placed on public property. Deputy sheriffs removed and confiscated the banners, claiming that they indicated disrespect for the flag of the United States and for county officials. The banners were kept by the sheriff's office, and the sheriff alleged that no request for their return was made by the union.

The Clash at La Casita

On December 28 a series of arrests began which continued through the next day. The initial arrest occurred at the site of La Casita farms, when Librado De La Cruz was arrested for allegedly striking an employee of La Casita Farms, Manuel Balli, as he was passing a group of union pickets in a pickup truck. Witnesses testified that Balli was not struck, that De La Cruz merely grasped Balli by his coat as the pickup slowly passed by while asking him to honor the union pickets. De La Cruz was allowed to go to the courthouse in his own vehicle, following the arresting officer, and the arresting officer did not file charges against De La Cruz. Instead, charges of preventing Balli from engaging in his lawful employment were preferred by an official of La Casita Farms. Four other picketers were charged with resisting arrest, additional charges of blocking a public road were brought against four of the picketers, and two strikers were charged with impersonating police officers. The last of these arrests was made because the two strikers had pinned shield-type badges to their shirts to identify themselves to the strikers as traffic aids to keep things orderly. Texas Rangers wear star-shaped badges and everyone knew what the shield badges meant. The authorities later dropped the charges and claimed the badges had been lost (Amicus brief in behalf of Medrano et al.).

On January 26, 1967, five union members were arrested while peacefully soliciting support for the employees of Trophy Farms. County officials alleged that the five were cursing local law enforcement officials through a loudspeaker in such a manner as to disturb the peace. On the same day, Reverend James Drake and Gilbert Padilla, vice president of the National Farm Workers Organizing Committee and one of the top assistants for César Chávez in California, were arrested following a prayer meeting on the courthouse grounds. Although most of the protesters had left the courthouse grounds, Drake and Padilla remained behind and were arrested for unlawful assembly. Testimony during the trial of *Medrano* v. *Allee* revealed that prior to the arrest of Drake and Padilla, the courthouse grounds had been used by various groups for night rallies, dances, and other similar gatherings (ibid.).

On February 1 four union members and five Roman Catholic priests were arrested and charged with disturbing the peace while urging workers in the La Casita fields to join the strike. The men claimed that they were on private property at the time of their arrest and that they were asking workers in the La Casita fields not to work for intolerably low wages and to cooperate with "La Causa." Among the priests arrested was Father William Killian, editor of the *Alamo Messenger*, the official Catholic newspaper of the Archdiocese of San Antonio. Father Killian and Father Sherrill Smith, social action director for the archdiocese, were disciplined by church officials for their failure to obtain ecclesiastical permission to go to Rio Grande City. However, the arrests of the two priests sparked an investigation by the Rio Grande valley office of the Federal Bureau of Investigation ("Boycott Mounts as FBI Probes Valley Arrests," *Alamo Messenger*, February 9, 1967, p. 1).

A Deadlocked Vote

On April 13 employees of Starr Produce packing sheds participated in a federally supervised election to determine whether or not the United Farm Workers Organizing Committee (UFWOC) would represent them in collective bargaining. Hopes ran high prior to the election, and the thirty workers who were to vote in the election were contacted individually by union organizers. "I'm sensing victory," Eugene Nelson stated, adding that the "vast majority indicated they are in favor of the union." He sounded a note of caution, however, noting that "you really never know until the votes are counted" ("Packing Shed Workers Vote Today on Union," *Alamo Messenger,* April 13, 1967, p. 1).

Nelson's caution was well founded, for when the votes were counted the election resulted in a fourteen-vote deadlock. Both the owners and the UFWOC filed complaints with the National Labor Relations Board over the disputed votes.

"The Private Police"

Events in May brought a confrontation between union officials and Captain Allee. On the morning of May 11 several of the union officials, including David López, were at the Camargo International Bridge supervising union pickets attempting to deter "green card" Mexican laborers from crossing the bridge in buses to take their places in the fields. López later told a reporter from the *Texas Observer* that, "a Ranger ignored his extended hand and 'pushed me roughly against my shoulders with both hands' " (Ronnie Dugger, "The Rangers and La Huelga," *Texas Observer,* June 9, 1967, p. 14).

The Rangers continued their harassment of the strikers. On May 12 they arrested nine demonstrators and charged them with disturbing the peace for shouting to workers in the La Casita fields and urging them to join the strike. On the same day, union leader Eugene Nelson became "quite perturbed" with Ranger harassment of the union organizers and went to the courthouse looking for Ranger Captain A. Y. Allee, who was in charge of the Rangers in the Rio Grande valley. Allee was not there, but Nelson had a confrontation with a deputy sheriff who later charged Nelson with threatening the lives of Rangers. Nelson claimed that he told the deputy that "if the Texas Rangers don't stop acting as the private police of La Casita, there are going to be some red-faced Rangers around here when the Senate investigators arrive." (Nelson was alluding to rumors that U.S. senators might come to investigate the situation in the valley.) Randall Nye, the county attorney, quoted the deputy, who was also an employee of La Casita Farms, as claiming that Nelson had told him, "You'd better tell that son of a bitch [Allee] he had better lay off or there's going to be some dead Rangers" (ibid., pp. 14–15).

A complaint was filed against Nelson for threatening the life of a peace officer; he was arrested later that afternoon, and bond was set at $2,000. Nelson's attorney tendered to a deputy sheriff a bond in the appropriate amount signed by Joseph Guerra, a wealthy local grower who had agreed to assume surety for the bond. The deputy refused the bond on Friday, but accepted it the following Monday after he had examined tax records and an affidavit showing that Guerra was one of seven heirs to his father's sizable estate. Later testimony showed that in the past Guerra had been accepted as surety for appearance bonds without presentation of tax records and the deputy testified that he personally knew Guerra to be a wealthy man.

The Climax of the Strike

Events leading to the climax of the strike were apparently triggered on Saturday, May 13, when the Mexican American Joint Conference, headed by the late Dr. George I. Sánchez of the University of Texas, meeting in Laredo, Texas, passed a series of resolutions. One of those resolutions, introduced by Bexar County Commissioner Albert Peña, criticized the Rangers for being used by "the State political establishment and local political machines as a vehicle to harass and terrorize the Mexican Americans" seeking their civil rights (Lupe Zamarripa, "UT, Rangers Hit by Peña," *Daily Texan,* May 16, 1967, p. 1). Peña criticized the Rangers for allegedly roughing up pickets and union leaders in Starr County and charged that the lawmen provide "comic relief for the rest of the nation in their cowboy boots, large hats, and larger pistols." In their resolutions, the members of the conference called for the Rangers to be dissolved (ibid.).

The Rangers continued to arrest large groups of strikers. On Thursday, May 18, the largest mass arrest to date resulted in twenty-two persons being taken to jail on misdemeanor charges of illegal picketing. Shortly afterward, the union was ordered to post no more pickets at Trophy Farms, site of the arrests, and State District Judge C. Woodrow Laughlin issued a temporary restraining order forbidding picketing by the union at the farms.

While the strikers were picketing the site, long lines of refrigerated cars waited on the tracks to carry the valley's multimillion-dollar melon crop to market. During the strike, cars driven by Texas Rangers escorted the trains carrying the melons. The Rangers insinuated that the train might possibly be derailed as tie plates and spikes had once been found on the tracks between Donna and Harlingen (ibid.).

While the strike was moving to its climax, the subcommittee of the Texas Advisory Committee to the United States Commission on Civil Rights held a closed-door hearing in Rio Grande City on May 25 and 26. Present at the hearings were: Garland Smith, attorney from Weslaco; Rafael H. Flores, attorney from McAllen; Albert Armendárez, attorney from El Paso; and Carlos Truan of Corpus Christi. Assisting was William B. Oliver, field representative from the Southern Field Office of the United States Commission on Civil Rights. Approximately thirty persons appeared before the subcommittee during the two days of hearings. Among them were representatives and members of the United Farm Workers Organizing Committee and the AFL–CIO; religious groups; private community organizations; attorneys for the union; attorneys for the growers; the county attorney, Randall Nye, who was also an attorney for Starr Produce Packing Shed; the district attorney; and others.

In its report, the subcommittee noted that

> Early in 1966, the UFWOC began a campaign in Starr County to organize persons employed by growers and packers.

Since the beginning of this drive, there have been reports alleging sabotage of farm machinery and other reports alleging physical violence. As a result of these allegations, the Starr County law enforcement officials requested the assistance of the Texas Rangers. About the time of the appearance of the Texas Rangers, the Committee began to receive requests to investigate allegations of denials of equal protection of the laws in the administration of justice. *(The Administration of Justice in Starr County,* report of the Subcommittee of the Texas Advisory Committee to the United States Commission on Civil Rights, June, 1967, p. 1 and passim)

The subcommittee also found that

members of UFWOC and other citizens active in the organizing campaign have been denied their legal rights in Starr County. These denials included:

1. Physical and verbal abuse by Texas Rangers and Starr County law enforcement officials;

2. Failure to bring promptly to trial members and union organizers against whom criminal charges have been alleged;

3. Holding of union organizers for many hours before they were released on bond;

4. Arrest of UFWOC members and organizers on the complaints of growers and packers without full investigation of the allegation in the complaints. In contrast, law enforcement officials made full investigations before acting on complaints filed by members and officers of UFWOC;

5. Encouragement of farm workers by Rangers to cross picket lines;

6. Intimidation by law enforcement officers of farm workers taking part in representation elections;

7. Harassment by Rangers of UFWOC members organizers, and a representative of the Migrant Ministry of the Texas Council of Churches which gave the appearance of being in sympathy with the growers and packers rather than the impartiality usually expected of law enforcement officers.

The majority of the farm workers and members of the Farm Workers Organizing Committee are Mexican Americans. To many Mexicans, the Texas Rangers are a symbol of oppression;

their appearance in Starr County only served to aggravate an already tense situation. While the committee supports fair and objective law enforcement agencies to seek outside assistance in this situation, it questions whether the Texas Rangers are the appropriate source for such assistance. (Ibid.)

Reverend Krueger and the Rangers

Three hours after the subcommittee closed its hearings, the Rangers arrested twelve persons picketing near a railroad track near Mission, Texas. Most of the picketers arrested had testified before the subcommittee ("Texas Rangers Arrest 12 Pickets Near Rail Site," *San Antonio Express-News,* May 27, 1967, p. 1). Most of the arrests were based on Texas laws, later challenged in court, dealing with picketing and unlawful assembly. The *Texas Observer* noted that the union's strategy was to have "information picket lines" at the railroad tracks for information only. The picketers announced that there was a strike, but did not advise anyone to refuse to patronize the railroad. The Rangers were using the Texas law against secondary picketing in this instance, taking the stance that the union was picketing the railroad, which was not a business that was being struck. The arrests were generally peaceful affairs, but there were several reported instances of violence (Dugger, "The Rangers and La Huelga," *Texas Observer,* June 9, 1967, p. 17).

Among the persons arrested on May 26 were the Reverend Ed Krueger, a member of a team ministry assigned to the valley by the Texas Council of Churches, and his wife. Krueger told a reporter for the *San Antonio Express-News* that he had been counseling the farmworkers not to attempt further picketing at a grade crossing in downtown Mission. While there, Krueger snapped a picture of Rangers who were watching a trainload of market-bound melons pass. He was arrested immediately. In giving his deposition later, Krueger related the incidents leading up to his arrest:

> As the train began to pass, I thought that it would make an interesting picture to show the Texas Rangers helping to get the train through town; and therefore, I snapped two or three pictures. A few seconds after the engine of the train had gone by Captain Allee walked over to me and said, "Krueger, you've been wanting to get arrested for a long time. I'm sick and tired of you." At that he very roughly grabbed me by the neck of my shirt, pulling it tight, and the seat of my pants and pushed me in the direction of the moving train. The newspaper reporters were on the north side of the train while the Rangers and several union members, many bystanders and myself were on the south side of the tracks at great distance from the train.
>
> While Captain Allee pushed me toward the moving train and was rough with me, my wife took a picture of what was happening. Then she too was arrested and her camera confiscated.
>
> Another Ranger grabbed Magdaleno Dimas, who had been sitting on the car eating his hamburger. Out in the middle of the street two Rangers began working Magdaleno over. One was holding him roughly and another Ranger yelled, "Get rid of that hamburger," and immediately slapped it out of his hand. After he slapped the hamburger out of his hands he reached back and seemingly with great aim and assuredly with all the force he could muster slapped Magdaleno in the face. Magdaleno gave no resistance at all. Nor did he say any word at all. The mark left on Magdaleno's cheek could be seen several hours later. Then they pushed Magdaleno over to the train which was still going by and held his face just a few inches from the train.
>
> After the train passed, they rushed Magdaleno toward the nearest Ranger car. A photographer took a picture and Captain Allee yelled, "Put that damn thing down or I'll take it away and send you to jail with them."
>
> When they got Magdaleno over to the car they threw him against it. His body hit the car with a loud thud. After searching him, he was pushed in the back seat of the car from the south side

and my wife pushed in from the north side. Just before this Doug Adair, who had been watching what was taking place, standing with his hands behind his back, was told, "You look like you want to be arrested too." Then he was pulled over to the south door of the car. I had just gotten into the car and was sitting on the edge of the seat in order to make room for Doug, who was being searched at that time. (Kemper Diehl, "Clergyman Charges Texas Rangers Too Rough," *San Antonio Express-News,* May 28, 1967, p. 15A)

Captain Allee later alleged that he arrested Krueger for "ramrodding much of the union's picketing." The captain alleged that he arrested Krueger because Krueger "asked to be arrested," stating that he told the minister: "This is the second time you have asked me to arrest you and I am sure as hell going to accommodate you." Texas Ranger Jack Van Cleve testified that he had arrested the minister's wife because she raised her arm and appeared to be preparing to strike Captain Allee with a camera she was holding in her hand. Van Cleve also stated that he nearly slapped Krueger when the minister got too close to him, as the minister had "bad breath" ("Ranger Tells About 'Dimas Incident,' "*San Antonio News,* June 14, 1968, p. 7B).

Krueger's arrest led the Texas Council of Churches to file suit against the Rangers, with the Texas Catholic Conference supporting the suit. According to the Associated Press,

The suit alleges the Rangers infringed upon the rights of observers in arresting the Kruegers. It alleges the Rangers "threatened, assaulted, falsely arrested and incarcerated persons . . . simply for being at the site of arrests, union activity and intended union activity." It asks the federal court to enjoin the Rangers from such activities in the future. (Paul Recer, Associated Press, "Texas Rangers Weathering Barrages of Criticism," *San Antonio News,* January 10, 1968, p. 1)

However, in 1969 the Texas Council of Churches announced that it was dropping the suit following a compromise agreement with state officials. Supposedly, the agreement assured that in the future the Rangers would respect the civil rights of the valley residents, but Reverend Krueger declined to sign the agreement on grounds that it exonerated the lawmen. Krueger was dismissed by the Texas Council of Churches shortly afterwards—the reason given for his dismissal was that there was need to change the operation in the valley ministry.

The Bernal Resolution

The mass arrests of striking farmworkers attracted nationwide publicity. Roy Reuther, citizenship director for the United Auto Workers union, telephoned protests to President Lyndon B. Johnson and Governor John Connally of Texas, citing the arrest of UAW representative Pancho Medrano at Mission and the $500 bond set for him on a charge that could only carry a maximum punishment of a $250 fine.

On Monday, May 29, 1967, State Senator Joe J. Bernal proposed a general investigating committee probe of Rangers' treatment of farmworkers and others involved in the striking, noting the arrest of Reverend Krueger and the long history of incidents involving the Rangers and Mexican Americans. Bernal's resolution asserted:

> it is being publicly alleged by various churchmen and interested citizens that the Texas Rangers are not impartially enforcing the laws of the state in connection with a labor dispute in the Rio Grande Valley, but are acting as partisan police force on the side of management . . . reports of incidents between Texas Rangers and picketing workers do have implications regarding Constitutional guarantees of freedom of speech, free assembly and the right of collective bargaining between labor and management that the Senate of Texas cannot ignore. (Senate Resolution presented before Texas Senate, May 29, 1967, pp. 1–2)

When Bernal attempted to introduce the resolution, other senators shouted down his efforts, calling further attention in the press to the plight of the striking farmworkers. Then Bernal, accompanied by a San Antonio television cameraman, made a dramatic visit to the Rio Grande valley to view the situation in person. Bernal's two-day visit brought him into direct confrontation with Ranger Captain Allee on two different occasions.

The Mexican-Americans' Ku Klux Klan

Shortly after he arrived in Rio Grande City, Senator Bernal went to the office of Justice of the Peace Brígido López to inquire about a union picket who had been held for fifteen hours without being charged. While Bernal was in the office, Captain Allee, accompanied by Ranger Sam Rogers, arrived. In the presence of Reverend Krueger, Allee, Rogers, several news media representatives, and the justice of the peace, Bernal asked Allee about arrest procedures, the Krueger arrests, and about the charges of unnecessary roughness on the part of the Rangers during the strike. Allee categorically denied any wrongdoing and told Krueger, in Bernal's presence, "Reverend Krueger, I never roughed you up." However, Krueger told Allee, "You did rough me up" ("Conversations with the Captain," *Texas Observer,* June 9, 1967, p. 22).

The meeting, which lasted forty-five minutes, began with polite fencing and degenerated into a shouting match "capped off by the captain's departure in a blaze of anger" (ibid.). At one point, the Ranger captain complained to Bernal that he (Bernal) had begun his visit to the valley by first going to the office of the strikers. Bernal replied that he had first gone to Ranger headquarters at the Ringgold Hotel. Since the Rangers were not there, he then went to the courthouse.

Later that day Bernal talked to several growers for about four hours at the First Methodist Church. Among the growers' complaints regarding activities of the union members was a statement by Ray Rochester, general manager of the La Casita Farm, who said he had spent more than $20,000 in the past year repairing vandalism caused by union members. He said he had received threatening telephone calls ("New Arrests of Pickets Stir Clash," *Valley Morning Star,* June 2, 1967, p. 1). Following the meeting, Bernal went to Mission where four pickets had been awaiting him. On his arrival they began picketing and were promptly arrested by the Rangers.

According to the *Texas Observer* account:

> Bernal said to Allee he'd always heard "one riot, one Ranger," but here it looked like four pickets, eight Rangers. Allee told him "I never thought I'd live to see the day some senator would come down here" and do as Bernal had. Bernal said he'd stick to being senator and Allee should stick to being a Ranger, and Allee said for him not to tell him what to stick to. Allee told reporters then, "I told him he had his flash, what he's looking for—he's got it."
>
> "I'm thoroughly convinced," Bernal said to reporters, that Allee is "on the side of the growers." Bernal did not think they should have come in at the request of the growers. The Rangers were correct legally in arresting people for secondary picketing, but had just violated Kathy Lynch's rights arresting her for this though she was not carrying a picket sign, he said. He thought the governor should call them out of the Valley and that despite the governor's saying he did not have this authority, he did. Did Bernal think the Rangers were acting as strikebreakers? "If they aren't, they're doing a darn good job at it" Bernal said. The Rangers, he concluded, are "the Mexican-Americans' Ku Klux Klan. All they need is a white hood with 'Rinches' written across it." ("Conversations with the Captain," p. 23)

Bernal's visit to the valley elicited more publicity, with United States Senator Ralph Yarborough claiming that the Ranger force had been misused by Governor Connally and that the force had been "turned from Texas Rangers to John Connally's strikebreakers" in the valley labor dispute (James McCrory, "Yarborough Claims Rangers 'Misused,'" *San Antonio Express,* May 29, 1967, p. 1).

Captain Allee had been called to Austin for a conference,

and on May 30, 1967, Governor Connally called a news conference and told reporters that the Rangers had been requested by local law enforcement officers in Starr County and that the force was there to enforce law and order and not for any other purpose. Connally also stated that "they were not ordered there by me and it was without any knowledge on my part until they were there." When asked if news reporters and photographers were being kept from reporting news happenings to the public, Connally replied that the Rangers are "not traditionally cast in the role of keeping reporters from telling the story of what happened. The Rangers have nothing to hide" ("The Public Debate," *Texas Observer*, June 9, 1967, p. 28).

The Dimas Incident

On Thursday, June 1, Captain Allee told Senator Bernal "I have never drawn one drop of blood here, skinned anyone's head or mistreated anyone. You blame me for enforcing the law. This is my territory and I'll continue to work here." Hours later the captain had a leading role in what came to be known as the "Dimas Incident," during which two strike supporters were injured while being arrested. The Dimas Incident received wide publicity throughout Texas and across the nation and resulted in public outcries against police brutality from many segments of society.

The Dimas Incident took its name from Magdaleno Dimas, an active member of the United Farm Workers Organizing Committee, who had been active in the strike and had been arrested with Reverend Krueger in Mission. Dimas was described by the *Texas Observer* as:

> A U.S. citizen, Mexico-born, 29-year-old Dimas is heavily tatooed. There is a dragon on his right arm, and there is a rose on his left arm.
>
> He was deported to Mexico in 1954, and four years later, Dimas was convicted of "murder without malice, assault to

murder," sentenced to five years from Wilson County, and evidently served three years. He was charged with driving without a license and passing on the right in Brownfield, and he paid a $25.50 fine there for being drunk. The record says he got a year in Starr County jail in 1963 for aggravated assault. That same year he was fined $100 and given three days for driving while drunk in Farwell, Texas. In 1965, at Del Rio and Lubbock, he was in trouble about smuggling aliens; the disposition is unclear from the record, but evidently he is on a probated sentence in this connection. The last entry of this kind is dated August 25, 1965. ("The Dimas Incident," *Texas Observer,* June 9, 1967, p. 23)

On the night of June 1, Captain Allee arrested Dimas and Benito Rodríguez after a long search that led to the house of Kathy Baker. The Rangers had searched all evening for Dimas to arrest him for allegedly brandishing a gun in a threatening manner in the presence of Special Deputy Jim Rochester at the La Casita Shed. Dimas later explained that he had been hunting rabbits, and when he could not find any, had shot a bird.

The Rangers found Dimas by tailing William Chandler and Alex Moreno to Kathy Baker's house with their car lights turned off. The Rangers had neither an arrest warrant nor a formal complaint on which a warrant could be based, so they put in a radio call for a justice of the peace and waited across the road. When Dimas emerged from the house with Chandler and Moreno, the Rangers moved toward them with their shotguns leveled. Captain Allee jabbed Moreno in the ribs with his shotgun, and the Rangers arrested both Moreno and Chandler, charging them with assisting Dimas to evade arrest. Dimas fled into the house after Chandler yelled at him to drop his gun, but the Rangers did not follow Dimas. Instead, they waited outside the house for the justice of the peace. When the justice of the peace arrived and signed the search warrant, the Rangers broke into the house and arrested both Dimas and Rodríguez. Captain Allee admitted that he struck Dimas on the head with his shotgun barrel once, but he testified in court a month later that neither man was hit or kicked at all except for that one blow. He also testified that both men fell when they attempted to run from the room and collided with a door and each other at the same time.

The four men were taken to the Starr County courthouse, and then to a medical clinic where they were treated by a male nurse, César Espinosa. When a doctor, Dr. Ramiro Casso examined Dimas, he told the *Observer*, "He was beaten out of his wits. Horrible. For somebody with a brain concussion to that extent to be in jail—that doesn't belong in this age at all" ("Medical and Press Matters," *Texas Observer,* June 9, 1967, p. 25). After Dr. Casso told reporters about Dimas's injuries, he and his wife received threatening telephone calls (ibid.).

Dimas was hospitalized from June 2 through June 6, and later court testimony revealed that Dimas

> suffered a brain concussion, multiple bruises on both sides of the neck and other bruises behind his left ear, on his left side, on the right side of his back, on his left forearm and left wrist. Dr. (Ramiro) Casso testified that x-ray negatives revealed that Dimas had received a severe blow to the lower right portion of his back causing the spine to curve out of shape away from the impact point. Dimas also sustained a laceration which required four stitches to close.
>
> Rodríguez had cuts and bruises behind his right ear, bruises on his right elbow, on his right upper arm, on the right upper portion of his back and on his right jaw. His left little finger was broken and the nail was torn off. (*Medrano* v. *Allee,* p. 617)

The court found it difficult "to visualize two grown men colliding with each other so as to cause such injuries" (ibid.). The details, however, were not known on the night of June 1, when the two bleeding men were in the Starr County courthouse. Senator Bernal was with Dimas shortly after the beating, and when reporters asked him how Dimas was, he was quoted as saying, "Well, he's as well as anyone who has been hit with a rifle on his head can be" ("Medical and Press Matters," p. 25).

However, the next day Colonel Homer Garrison, Jr., director of the Texas Department of Public Safety, issued a three-page statement denying the allegations of Ranger brutality. He said charges of brutality by police were the "common defense and cry of a professional criminal and agitator. . . . The very simple answer to those critics of the Texas Rangers is this: if they will only obey the law, no Texas Ranger ever has or ever will molest them" ("The Public Debate," p. 28).

On June 3, Senator Bernal sent a letter of complaint to Governor Connally asking him to remove the Ranger force from the valley. He cited four violations of civil rights he had seen committed by the Rangers, among them Dimas's arrest (letter, Senator Joe J. Bernal to Governor John B. Connally, June 3, 1967, files of Joe J. Bernal). However, Colonel Garrison sent Bernal a resume of the Ranger activities which stated that

> on June 1, Captain Allee and Ranger Dawson, after receiving a call from the Sheriff's Office in Rio Grande City regarding two subjects reportedly seen with a rifle, located the suspects, Magdaleno Dimas and Benito Rodríguez, at a house occupied by Kathy Baker. After being instructed by Judge Lopez to arrest the suspects, and after the suspects refused to open the door, Captain Allee forceably entered the house and after some resistance arrested Dimas and Rodríguez on charges of Displaying a Deadly Weapon and Disturbance of the Peace. (Letter, Colonel Homer Garrison to Senator Joe Bernal, June 7, 1967, files of Joe J. Bernal)

The Strike Collapses

After the Dimas Incident the strike gradually lost its momentum. Several factors led to the decline of the strike. The high number of arrests and the heavy fines imposed were cutting deeply into limited union funds. Wages for farm work in the valley had risen from fifty cents to $1.25 per hour, giving many workers reason to cease picketing. Intimidation of strikers engendered fear of participation. Despite support from numerous groups and from the union, many farmworkers were afraid to picket with the Rangers watching their activities. The union was also unable to prevent "green card" workers from Mexico from crossing the International Bridge to take the jobs in the fields that striking workers left. Finally, the campaign to discredit the union by accusing it or its members of violence and sabotage was effective in causing a crippling lack of support for the union. During the strike the union was blamed for burning a railroad trestle; stacking tie plates and stakes in the railroad right of way; causing about $20,000 in damages by vandalism at La Casita Farm, including the burning of buildings and trucks; putting sugar into gas tanks; slashing tires; and violating a number of state laws.

The steady pressure on the strike finally resulted in its collapse. On June 28, after two days of testimony, State District Judge C. W. Laughlin issued a temporary injunction prohibiting all picketing at La Casita Farms. The melon crop was picked and shipped with little economic damage to the growers. While the strike did not accomplish all it set out to do, it did call attention to the plight of the agricultural workers in the Rio Grande valley and did give impetus to the political movement that led to the founding of La Raza Unida.

Medrano v. *Allee*

The most important event in the cause of justice for the farmworkers of Texas and the exposure of the Rangers came with the adjudication of the *Medrano* v. *Allee* case five years after the strike.

On June 26, 1972, a three-judge federal court met in Brownsville to hear a class action suit first filed in state court in 1967 on behalf of Francisco Medrano and other farmworkers.

In its decision, the panel struck down two civil and three criminal statutes of the state which had been the basis of action against the union pickets. These statutes dealt with mass picketing; unlawful assembly; abusive language; secondary picketing, striking, and boycott; and disturbing the peace. The court also noted that the net result of maintaining law and order was that the law had taken sides in what had started as mainly a labor-employer dispute. The court further noted that the arrests, detentions without filing of charges, and threats of further prosecution of pro-union activities did not cease.

However, the case was appealed to the Supreme Court and heard by the Court on November 13, 1973. On May 20, 1974, Justice William O. Douglas read the majority opinion.

The U.S. Supreme Court:
Allee et al. v. *Medrano et al.*

The wheels of justice grind slowly. As noted earlier, on June 28, 1967, a state district judge issued a temporary injunction prohibiting all picketing at La Casita Farms. Shortly thereafter the farmworkers filed a class action suit against the Rangers. The case was not heard until 1972 when the three-judge federal panel ruled in favor of the farmworkers. The case was appealed to the Supreme Court, heard in 1973, and decided in 1974, seven years after the filing of the original suit.

In the original suit the farmworkers attacked the constitutionality of certain Texas statutes and alleged that the Rangers and other officers conspired to deprive them of their first and fourteenth amendment rights. The federal district court declared five of the statutes unconstitutional and permanently enjoined the Rangers and other officers from intimidating the farmworkers in their organizational efforts. In specifying what was meant by intimidation, the court prohibited the defendants from using their authority as peace officers to arrest, stop, disperse, imprison, or otherwise interfere with workers' organizational efforts without adequate cause. The Supreme Court agreed with the opinion of the district court:

> Because of the intimidation by State authorities, their lawful effort was crushed. The workers, and their leaders and organizers were placed in fear of exercising their constitutionally protected rights of free expression, assembly, and association. . . . Where, as here, there is a persistent pattern of police misconduct, injunctive relief is appropriate. (*Allee* v. *Medrano,* pp. 814–815)

> In this blunderbuss effort the police [Rangers] not only relied on statutes the District Court found constitutionally deficient, but concurrently exercised their authority under valid laws in an unconstitutional manner. (Ibid., p. 812)

The factual findings of the district court were not challenged by the Supreme Court. Most of these findings have been mentioned throughout the present chapter.

In the adjudication of this case the "vigorous" methods of the Texas Rangers were fully exposed. Also exposed was the use of their authority in an unconstitutional manner. It was also clear that the law enforcement officials took sides in what was a labor-management controversy and that the maintenance of law and order was inextricably bound to preventing the success of the strike. Thus the cause of justice for the farmworkers was served, albeit too late to affect the organizing efforts of 1967.

A Relic of a Primitive Age
in Texas

To WRITE ABOUT the Rangers, regardless of viewpoint, is to touch emotion, especially in current times. To strike a balance between the two opposing views of the Texas Rangers would be to have had the Chief Justice of the United States Supreme Court read the 1974 opinion from a podium in the new Texas Ranger Hall of Fame.

From the origin of the Texas Rangers in 1840 to the present time, the purpose and methods of the Rangers have been points of controversy. Throughout most of their history they have been a poorly trained and ineffective law enforcement agency. There is no evidence that the Texas Rangers can hold claim to having enforced Texas law in an impartial manner whenever an ethnic person or group is involved.

The Texas Rangers and the legends handed down through the generations in extravagant terms are manifestations of that strain of Americanism which our country has correctly identified as racism. The Texas Ranger is the law-and-order, cactus-and-tumbleweed version of Horatio Alger—white, self-sufficient, the most rugged of rugged individuals, possessing in abundance virtues that all men aspire to; in short, the most perfect entity to preserve and protect all that is good, decent, and honest against contamination by alien peoples or philosophies. The system and attitude that created the Texas Ranger and attendant mythology have for too long been protected under the brim of the proverbial ten-gallon white hat. What is under that hat are the interests of a white-skinned power structure.

It is the system in control of Ranger conduct, not necessarily the individual Ranger, that has provoked considerable concern. The adjutant generals who have failed or even refused to investigate obvious wrongdoing among their subordinates, the governors who have either disclaimed Ranger actions or insisted that they are only enforcing the law, the directors of the Department of Public Safety who have been less than candid with the public, the superiors of the Rangers who have permitted their officers to be used as instruments of the prevailing power structures—these are the offices and individuals who must justify the existence of the Rangers and their behavior.

In recent times the use of the technique "stonewalling it" has taught America a hard lesson: the stone wall is there to hide something. What has been hidden behind the wall of silence is a special police unit which is given authority to perform functions that are contrary to the American commitment to equal rights and justice for all men. It is wholly proper and essential to ask and receive an answer to the question: What are the Texas Rangers if they are not the exclusive police arm of white Texas politicians and men of money seeking to perpetuate the oppression of minorities to further their own supremacy and financial gain?

Any proposal that the Texas Rangers be abolished anticipates opposition from a large segment of the Texas population, who, rooted deeply in Texas history and tradition and all its symbols, would react as if it were a suggestion to bulldoze the Alamo to make way for a parking lot. On the other hand, those who have been at the receiving end of the Texas Rangers' power and have seen the force as a symbol of what is wrong with Texas would welcome their disappearance.

Texas is a state that prides itself on its myths. The Rangers remain among the most anachronistic of the myths that surround the Great Lone Star State. The Texas Rangers no longer exist as a symbol of law and order to many citizens of Texas; and in the Rio Grande valley, they stand as a symbol of oppression.

However, despite the fact that numerous state officials, political candidates, reporters, and concerned citizens of the state have called for the abolishment of the Rangers, the Ranger force remains the primary symbol of law and order to conservative groups around the state. During the farmworkers' strike in Rio Grande City, U.S. Senator Ralph Yarborough called the Rangers "a relic of a primitive age in Texas" ("Shock Waves from Popeye Land," *Texas Observer,* May 16, 1963, p. 1). However, Yarborough, along with Governor Dolph Briscoe, U.S. Senator Lloyd Bentsen, and other state officials, joined retired Rangers and members of the current force in saluting the Ranger tradition at the opening of their museum in Waco in 1976. When Frances Farenthold, while campaigning for governor of Texas as a reform candidate in 1972, called for the abolishment of the Rangers, she received hundreds of telephone calls supporting the force, and the issue proved to be one of the most unpopular of her campaign.

The Modern Texas Ranger

The qualifications for a Texas Ranger have changed drastically since the early days of the frontier. In 1824 the only qualifications for a "ranging man" were a good horse, a rifle, and a strong sense of survival. In 1976 the qualifications were numerous:

> each applicant must be at least 30 and less than 50 years of age, a citizen of the United States of America, in excellent physical condition and have an outstanding record of at least 8 years experience with a bona fide law enforcement agency engaged principally in the investigation of major crime; applicants must have a background subject to a thorough investigation which would reflect good moral character and habits and must not have a conviction for any felony crime within this state or elsewhere;

an applicant must possess a valid Texas operator, commercial operator, or chauffeur's license and any previous conviction for Driving While Intoxicated or Driving Under the Influence of Drugs will automatically reject; applicants must have completed high school or submit a certificate showing an equivalent educational background which is acceptable according to Texas Education Agency standards; applicants will be required to pass a thorough physical examination. . . . Applicant must produce an "Intermediate Certificate" in law enforcement awarded by the Texas Commission on Law Enforcement Officers Standards and Education. (form letter from W. D. Wilson, Senior Ranger Captain, Texas Ranger Service, Texas Department of Public Safety, sent to all applicants applying to join the Texas Ranger Service)

Captain Bill Wilson, who handles all public relations and inquiries to Ranger headquarters, says that an additional requirement has been added to the list—sixty hours of college work. When asked if the requirement tended to exclude any persons from applying for service with the force, Captain Wilson stated that the college requirement tended to eliminate many Mexican Americans and other minority members who might otherwise qualify for Ranger service (interview, W. D. Wilson).

According to Captain Wilson, the federal government guidelines required the Rangers to omit a previous requirement, a provision that each applicant "must be not less than 68 inches nor more than 76 inches in height, weight not less than two pounds per inch of height nor more than three and one-half pounds per inch of height" (form letter, Ranger Headquarters).

Captain Wilson gives a very lucid review of the ways in which the Rangers operate within the state and how they cooperate with local law enforcement agencies. "We are set up under statute as an assisting agency to aid local personnel. We are usually called in by local law enforcement officers, but sometimes we initiate action ourselves," Captain Wilson says. The captain sees the Texas Ranger's role in law enforcement activities as fourfold: "the investigation of major crimes, the apprehension of fugitives, the suppression of riots and insurrections, and the protection of life and property" (interview, Captain W. D. Wilson).

One facet of Ranger activities is seldom publicized. According to Captain Wilson, any private citizen can call for help from the Texas Rangers and some do. However, as he points out, it is customary for the citizen to appeal to local law enforcement officers and have them ask for help from the Rangers. Then, the Rangers can work with the local authorities or assist as an outside agency. Although the local law enforcement agencies have the first responsibility to citizens in their communities, Captain Wilson points out that the Rangers "do not have to stop and ask permission of local law enforcement officers" before entering a county on behalf of its citizens (ibid.).

The Special Rangers

Another group of Texas Rangers that is equally anachronistic and as seldom publicized is a force known as Special Rangers. More than any other body of the force, the Special Rangers continue to represent the nineteenth-century frontier tradition and to serve the conservative interests of the state of Texas. R. B. Wilson has been a Special Ranger for eight years, and is one of the thirty-two Special Rangers who work for various interests throughout Texas and Oklahoma and are not paid by state funds. Wilson (who is not related to Senior Ranger Captain W. D. Wilson) works as a special agent for the Texas and Southwestern Cattle Raisers Association, an organization that boasts among its membership some of the wealthiest cattle raisers in the state. One of the organization's honorary past presidents is Richard M. Kleberg, Jr., of the renowned King Ranch, and one of its past presidents is Texas Governor Dolph Briscoe, Jr. *(The Cattleman,* February 9, 1976, p. 19).

Although R. B. Wilson has never been a Texas Ranger, he became a Special Ranger through his work as a market inspector at auction sales. Now he patrols nine adjoining counties working for the cattle raisers and looking for evidence of cattle or horse rustling. According to Special Ranger Wilson, horse rustling in Texas has become big business, with horse rustlers making off with not only the horse, but also with expensive horse gear and trailers (interview, Ann Fears Crawford with Special Ranger R. B. Wilson, Ranger Headquarters, Austin, February 4, 1976).

Cattle rustling, widespread during the early days of the Texas frontier, has made a comeback. According to Wilson, "If more cattlemen branded their cattle and recorded their brands with the county clerk, there would be less cattle rustling in the state" (ibid.).

Special Ranger Wilson sees his job as all part of the general need for law and order in the state of Texas. He believes that the apprehension of criminals is what he's there for, and he feels that new laws are often too soft on criminals. He feels that reading a criminal about to be arrested his rights is ridiculous. "I don't believe in police brutality," he says, "but I do believe in getting his attention" (ibid.).

The Governor and the Rangers

Under the Texas constitution, the governor is a relatively weak executive, and in recent years one of his most controversial acts has been "calling out the Rangers." During the 1970s, this reaction has been due to the publicity surrounding the incidents in Crystal City and Rio Grande City. Texas governors have been relatively hesitant to send the Rangers into the Rio Grande valley. When asked what kind of possible altercations between Rangers and Mexican Americans might cause him to call out the Rangers, Governor Dolph Briscoe, cautious in all public relations matters, failed to respond to the question.

Texas Attorney General John L. Hill, through Mary Jane Bode, his assistant for information, responded to the same inquiry with copies of recent opinions concerning the governor's use of the Rangers. However, in answering specific questions about situations where the governor's powers relative to use of the Rangers would be employed, Hill stated that, "he can't 'anticipate' what the governor would do" (letter, Mary Jane Bode, Assistant for Information, Attorney General of Texas, to Ann Fears Crawford, March 29, 1976. Letter in files of Dr. Julian Samora).

Although the climate of opinion has changed somewhat from the 1960s to the 1970s, the governor's right to call in the Rangers remains inviolate. However, since John Connally left the governor's mansion in 1969, Texas governors have failed to live up to Connally's ideas of a "strong executive" (Crawford and Keever, 1973, p. 219). Should the governor desire to send in the Rangers, his right to do so rests in Article 4, Section 10, of the Constitution of the State of Texas. Attorney General's Opinion No. 0-2662, approved on September 5, 1940, clarifies the constitutionality of the law that placed the Texas Rangers as a separate division under the Department of Public Safety. The opinion states that the governor is not required to execute the laws of the state, but only to see that proper state officials do execute such laws (Opinion No. 0-2662, Attorney General of Texas, September, 5, 1940). However, according to this opinion, only in exceptional circumstances may the governor call out the militia to bring about faithful execution of the laws (ibid.). These "exceptional circumstances" are certainly open to reinterpretation in the 1970s.

The attorney general's opinion relating to Special Rangers also clarify the role of these employees. Opinion No. M-966, approved October 6, 1971, sets out the standards of selection and training of Special Rangers:

> Employees of statewide organizations who have been appointed special rangers by the Public Safety Commission to

promote cooperation between their offices and the various law enforcement offices throughout the state, are peace officers and must comply with established minimum standards of selection and training, as established by the Texas Commission on Law Enforcement Officer Standards and Education.

A later opinion points out the persons who may be appointed as Special Rangers:

> The office of Special Ranger is an office in the executive branch of the government and appointment of an elected judge or a state Legislator to be a Special Ranger would violate Article 2, Section 1, of the constitution. Designation of an appointed member of the staff of an elected member of the Legislature likewise would be violative of Article 2, Section 1, of the constitution.
>
> An elected member of the executive department of the government of the State of Texas may be appointed a Special Ranger provided there is no incompatibility between the office of the appointee and the office of Special Ranger. (Attorney General's Opinion No. H-7, February 12, 1973, p. 29)

In light of these opinions and the recent revisions in the qualifications for both peace officers and Texas Rangers, some Special Rangers now operating in Texas are not qualified to do so.

Some Important Questions

During the period of research for this work the authors met on several occasions to discuss the issues being uncovered. A number of questions were being raised which helped guide the research and we felt that in providing answers to them one could come to a better understanding of the subject matter of this essay. The questions posed were:

1. What truth or fabrication is there to the historical accounts woven into the Ranger image?

2. To which segments of the population do the Rangers respond?

3. Have the Rangers been defenders of the democratic political process?

4. To whom are the Rangers responsible?

5. What has been the relationship of the Rangers to existing power structures?

6. How are the Rangers selected? What qualifications are required for service in the force?

7. What is the proper function or service of the Rangers today?

8. Do they duplicate the services of other law enforcement officers (municipal, county, and state) in Texas?

9. Have the Rangers engaged in strikebreaking?

10. Have they violated the civil rights of Texas citizens?

11. What has been the response of the superiors (adjutant generals, governors, directors of the Department of Public Safety) when criticism or legal charges have been leveled against the Rangers?

In providing answers to the above questions a number of themes became apparent:

The Rangers were organized not only to suppress law-breakers, but to suppress already oppressed minorities—both Indian and Mexican—in the wake of Anglo-American settlement. The oppression of minorities continued through the 1960s.

The Rangers have historically been a lawless breed of men who have had law and order on their side.

The myth of the "super-lawman"—the fighter for law and order—has ridden with the Rangers in the past and still rides with them today.

The power structure in the state of Texas has used the Texas Rangers to maintain the status quo and to maintain both its economic and its political position in the state.

The activities of the Rangers throughout the state of Texas

have given impetus to a rise in organization for political action among Mexican Americans. This was particularly evident in the 1960s.

Conclusions and Recommendations

After reevaluating the myth of the Rangers in the light of historical accuracy and in the light of the political realities of the 1970s, the authors find that it would be a hard task to evade the conclusion that the Texas Rangers are an anachronism in any kind of civilized society, and that they have indeed outlived what usefulness they once had. But romantic images die hard, especially when we have scholars of the stature of Webb and political figures like Lyndon Baines Johnson and Richard Milhous Nixon lending the prestige of their position to further the Ranger legend.

The Texas Rangers duplicate the functions of most law enforcement officers in Texas. The law permits local, municipal, and county police officers to enter into cooperative agreements in situations deemed beyond the control of a local unit. The law permits deputizing of others in serious situations. Since there are other law enforcement agencies beyond the local level, such as the Headquarters Division, the highway patrol and the National Guard, what is the need for a ninety-four-man Texas Ranger force and the "honorific" Special Ranger force?

It is a matter of historical record that the Rangers have operated without restraint and with seemingly unchecked power. This power has been abused under the guise of maintaining law and order; unchecked power invariably will be abused. This agency has never been responsible to a local electorate as have sheriffs and policemen. It is a matter of historical record that the Rangers have been brutal (Webb would say "vigorous") in their methods of upholding *their* interpretation of law and in their violations of the civil rights of citizens. More recently they have interfered in the local political process and in the organizing activities of farmworkers, actually serving as strikebreakers. All of this is part of the pattern of protecting the controlling economic interests.

The Ranger image has had an unfavorable effect on Texas law enforcement by providing a colorful but antiquated model for constables, sheriffs, deputies, and other policemen and by being a symbol of arbitrary and at times brutal methods in the eyes of a growing number of Texas citizens.

Since the Rangers have no real or perhaps unique or separate function as a law enforcement body, since they duplicate other law enforcement bodies, perhaps they could be given a unique function, that of a colorful guard assisting in the ceremonial functions of the governor; or of guards at state parks, zoos and museums, particularly the new Ranger museum in Waco.

If the selection process were more objective, nonpolitical, and unbiased as to the criteria of race and national origin, perhaps a new generation of Rangers would gain more credibility in the eyes of the oppressed.

If they were made accountable in a more direct way to the local authorities and citizenry this might curtail the abuse of power.

Higher qualifications, better pay, uniforms, and marked cars might enhance the force.

Many people believe, and some have so stated, that as long as there is a Texas there will always be Texas Rangers. This may be so. But as long as the myths remain unchallenged and the behavior of the Rangers remains unchanged, they will be perceived by many, not as heroes, but as oppressors.

In order to implement a program by which conditions between Texans—both Anglo and Mexican-American—can be worked out without the intervention of the Texas Rangers, we suggest various alternatives to the problem of "sending in the Rangers." These are:

1. As members of the press have suggested, the Rangers may be abolished as a distinct outfit, and members of the force

transferred into the Department of Public Safety's corps of officers (Dugger, *Texas Observer,* May 9, 1969, p. 3).

2. Changes in statutes can be implemented by which the Texas Rangers may not be called into an area unless specifically requested by local law enforcement officers.

3. An advisory board, composed of law enforcement officials, minority members, and experts in both minority and legal affairs, can be constituted to advise the governor of Texas as to when it might be expedient to send in a Ranger force and when a potentially explosive situation can best be handled by local law enforcement officers.

4. The governor of the state of Texas can call together a commission to study the use of the Texas Rangers in law enforcement activities in the state. This commission should be composed of law enforcement officials, minority members, members of local law enforcement agencies, and others deemed necessary to make an impartial study of the role of the Rangers and to suggest alternative solutions to the problems that have been created and to suggest alternatives to the duplication of law enforcement roles now in evidence.

5. It could be required that all members of law enforcement groups within the state of Texas, as part of their training program, take an intensive course in human relations, including work that deals with methods of working with minority groups.

6. As the Texas Rangers form an "elite corps" among law enforcement groups in Texas, the wisest course of action might be to relegate the force to ceremonial status. Then, instead of serving as a group in conflict with local law enforcement agencies, the Ranger force would constitute an honorary corps to attend state functions and to fulfill their historic role as an integral part of the "frontier tradition" of the Great Lone Star State.

Bibliography

Books and Articles

Adams, Ramon. 1967. *The Cowman and His Philosophy*. Austin, Tex.: Encino Press.

Banks, C. S. and McMillan, G. T., eds. 1947, 1960. *The New Texas Reader*. San Antonio: Tex.: Naylor Company.

Barker, Eugene Campbell. 1925. *The Life of Stephen F. Austin: Founder of Texas, 1793–1836: A Chapter in the Westward Movement of the Anglo-American People*. Nashville and Dallas: Cokesbury Press.

Connor, Seymour U. 1971. *Texas: A History*. New York: Thomas Y. Crowell.

Crawford, Ann Fears, and Keever, Jack. 1973. *John B. Connally: Portrait in Power*. Austin, Tex.: Jenkins Publishing Company.

Day, Donald. 1947. *Big Country: Texas*. New York: Duell, Sloan & Pearce.

Dobie, J. Frank, ed. 1966. *Tone the Bell Easy*. Dallas: Southern Methodist University Press, 1932; facsim. reprint, 1966.

Elliott, Keith. 1973. "Texas Department of Public Safety." *Texas Parade*, August.

Fehrenbach, T. R. 1968. *Lone Star: A History of Texas and the Texans*. New York: Macmillan.

Fidler, Paul E. 1935. "A State Police Force for Texas." *Texas Municipalities* 22, no. 3 (March).

Forbis, William H. 1973. *The Cowboys*. New York: The Editors of Time-Life.

Ford, John S. 1963. *Rip Ford's Texas*. Ed. Stephen B. Oates. Austin, Tex.: University of Texas Press.

Friend, Llerena B. 1971. "W. P. Webb's Texas Rangers." *Southwestern Historical Quarterly* 74, no. 3 (January).

Frost, H. Gordon, and Jenkins, John H. 1968. *I'm Frank Hamer: The Life of a Texas Peace Officer*. Austin, Tex.: Pemberton Press.

Gillett, James B. 1925. *Six Years with the Texas Rangers: 1875–1881*. Ed. M. M. Quaife. New Haven, Conn.: Yale University Press.

Goldstein, Kenneth S. 1964. "The Texas Rangers in Aberdeenshire." In Mody C. Boatright, et al., *A Good Tale and a Bonnie Tune*. Dallas: Southern Methodist University Press.

Harris, Charles H., III. 1964. *The Sanchez Navarros: A Socio-Economic Study of a Coahuilan Latifundio 1846–1853*. Chicago: Loyola University Press.

Horgan, Paul. 1968. *Great River: The Rio Grande in North American History*. New York, Chicago, San Francisco: Holt, Rinehart and Winston.

Institute for Educational Development. 1973. *The Chicano Almanac*. San Antonio, Tex.

Katz, Harney. 1972. *Shadow on the Alamo*. Garden City, N.Y.: Doubleday.

Lasswell, Mary. 1958. *I'll Take Texas*. New York: Houghton Mifflin.

McClesky, Clifton. 1972. *The Government and Politics of Texas*. Boston: Little, Brown.

Morris, Margaret Francine, comp. 1968. "Walter Prescott Webb, 1888–1963: A Bibliography." In William F. Holmes, ed., *Essays on the American Civil War* by Frank E. Vandiver, Martin Hardwick Hall, Homer L. Kerr. Austin, Tex.: University of Texas Press.

Nimmo, Dan, and Oden, William E. 1971. *The Texas Political System*. Englewood Cliffs, N.J.; Prentice-Hall.

Oswandel, J. J. 1885. *Notes of the Mexican War, 1846-47-48*. Philadelphia.

Paine, Albert Bigelow. 1909. *Captain Bill McDonald, Texas Ranger: A Story of Frontier Reform*. New York: J. J. Little & Ives Company.

Paredes, Américo. 1958. *With His Pistol in His Hand*. Austin, Tex.: University of Texas Press.

———. 1963. "El Cowboy Norteamericano en el Folklore y la Literatura." *Folklore Americano* 4.

————. 1971. "The United States, Mexico, and *Machismo*." *Journal of the Folklore Institute* 8, no. 1.

Pierce, Frank C. 1917. *A Brief History of the Lower Rio Grande Valley*. Menasha, Wis.: George Banta Publishing Company.

Prassel, Frank R. 1972. *The Western Peace Officer*. Norman, Okla.: University of Oklahoma Press.

Proctor, Ben H. 1970. "The Modern Texas Rangers: A Law Enforcement Dilemma in the Rio Grande Valley." In Manuel P. Servín, ed., *The Mexican Americans: An Awakening Minority*. Beverly Hills, Calif.: Glencoe Press. (Proctor's article was originally published in John A. Carroll, ed., *Reflections of Western Historians*. Tucson: University of Arizona Press, 1969.)

Reid, Samuel C., Jr. 1848. *The Scouting Expeditions of McCulloch's Texas Rangers*. Philadelphia: G. B. Zieber and Company.

Richardson, Rupert Norval. 1943. *Texas: The Lone Star State*. New York: Prentice-Hall.

Shockley, John Staples. 1974. *Chicano Revolt in a Texas Town*. Notre Dame, Ind.: University of Notre Dame Press.

Sims, Judge Orland L. 1967. *Gunfighters I Have Known*. Austin, Tex.: Encino Press.

Steen, Ralph W. 1960. *The Texas Story*. Rev. ed. Austin, Tex.: Steck Company.

Sterling, William Warren. 1959. *Trails and Trials of a Texas Ranger*. Norman, Okla.: University of Oklahoma Press.

Weaver, John. 1973. *The Brownsville Raid*. New York: Norton Publishers.

Webb, Walter Prescott. 1935; rev. ed. 1965. *The Texas Rangers: A Century of Frontier Defense*. Boston and New York: Houghton Mifflin. Rev. ed., Dallas: University of Texas Press.

————, ed. 1952. *The Handbook of Texas*. Austin, Tex.: Texas State Historical Association.

Government Reports

Proceedings of the Joint Committee of the Senate and House in the Investigation of the Texas State Ranger Force. 1919. Texas State Archives, Austin.

Report of the Joint Legislative Committee on Organization and Economy and Griffenhagen and Associates. Part III. General Executive and Administrative Agencies, and the Militia, Texas Rangers, Highway Patrol, and Examining Boards. January 10, 1933, Austin, Tex.

United States Commission on Civil Rights. February 1970. *A Report of the Texas Advisory Committee to the United States Commission on Civil Rights.*

Newspapers

Alamo Messenger (San Antonio).

Austin American-Statesman.

Corpus Christi Caller-Times.

Daily Texan (Austin).

Dallas Morning News.

San Antonio Express-News.

San Antonio Herald.

San Antonio Light.

Texas Observer (Austin).

Valley Morning Star.

Interviews

Albert Peña, Jr., with Albert Fuentes, San Antonio, May 23, 1973.

Albert Peña, Jr., with Martin García, Houston, June 12, 1973.

Albert Peña, Jr., with José Angel Gutierrez, San Antonio, May 19, 1973.

Albert Peña, Jr., with Severita Lara, San Antonio, July 10, 1973.

Albert Peña, Jr., with Henry Muñoz, San Antonio, March 16, 1973.

Ann Fears Crawford with Special Ranger R. B. Wilson, Austin, February 4, 1976.

Ann Fears Crawford with Ranger Captain W. D. Wilson, Austin, February 4, 1976.

Unpublished Material

Bustamante, Jorge A., and Samora, Julian. 1971. "The Texas Rangers: Heroes or Oppressors?" Paper presented at the 66th Annual Meeting of the American Sociological Association, Denver, Colo., August 30–September 2.

Crawford, Ann Fears. 1971. "Mexican-Texan Relations During the Ferguson Years." Chapter of projected book.

Charlton, Thomas Lee. 1971. "The Texas Department of Public Safety." Master's thesis, University of Texas.

Schuster, Stephen W. 1965. "The Modernization of the Texas Rangers." Master's thesis, Texas Christian University.

Webb, Walter Prescott. "Chapter XXIV, The Texas Rangers in the Modern World: 1935–1960." Incomplete ms. Walter Prescott Webb Collection Archives, Eugene C. Barker, Texas History Center. University of Texas, Austin, n.d.

Index

A

Albidress, Charlie, 103
Allee, Captain A. Y., 91, 93, 96,
    102, 104–107, 111, 114–116,
    118, 128, 131, 140, 145–146,
    148–150
Allee, Alfred Y., Jr., 92, 106
Allee, Tom, 116, 120
Allred, Governor James V., 77,
    79, 80
Apaches, 16, 20, 36, 53, 54
Arredondo, Domingo, 136
Austin, Moses, 17
Austin, Stephen F., 17

B

Baker, Sergeant A. Y., 56, 57
Baker, Kathy, 151
Barnes, Ben, 134
Bastrop, Baron de, 17
Bentsen, Senator Lloyd, 159
Bernal, Senator Joe J., 13, 147,
    148, 150, 152, 153
Billings, John, 126
Brazos River, 17
Briscoe, Governor Dolph, 159,
    161, 162
Brown, Hank S., 135
Burleson, General Edward, 24
Byrd, Colonel D. Harold, 123

C

Callahan, J. H., 36

Callicott, Bill, 49, 52
Canales, J. T., 12, 66
Cárdenas, Antonio, 101, 114, 116
Carmichael, Colonel Horace H.,
    82
Carr, Attorney General Waggoner,
    116, 117, 134
Casso, Dr. Ramiro, 152
Chandler, William, 151
Chávez, César, 132, 135, 139
Cherokees, 16, 21, 22
Citizens Committee for Better
    Government, 99
Ciudadanos Unidos, 127
Clemens, Jeremiah, 39
Coke, Richard, 47
Colorado River, 17
Colquitt, Governor Oscar B., 61,
    63
Comanches, 16, 20, 22, 23, 32, 33
Connally, Governor John B., 13,
    116, 117, 133–135, 147, 149,
    150, 153, 163
Cornejo, Juan, 98, 99, 101, 107,
    112, 114, 115, 117, 118, 120,
    123
Cortez, Gregorio, 58–61
Cortinas, Juan Nepomuceno, 34,
    35, 37, 38, 47
Cortinas War, 33–37
Crawford, Ann Fears, 86, 162, 163
Crystal City, Texas, 87, 89–91
Cruz, Bob, 117

D

Davenport, Judge Harbert, 6
Davis, Governor E. J., 47
Davis, Jefferson, 32
De La Cerda, Ramon, 57
De La Cruz, Librado, 138
De La Cruz, Reynaldo, 137
Del Monte Corporation, 89
Department of Public Safety. *See*
    Texas Department of Public
    Safety.
Dickens, Andrew, 98
Dill, James, 103, 116, 118
Dimas, Magdaleno, 145, 150–152
Dixie, Chris, 115, 116
Dixon, Captain N. K., 83
Dobie, J. Frank, 41
Drake, Reverend James, 138, 139

E

"El Corrido de Gregorio Cortez,"
    58
Elgin, John, 13, 69
Elgin v. *Neff*, 68, 69, 76
Evans, Roy, 13

F

Falcón, Moses, 94, 95
Farenthold, Frances, 159
Ferguson, James E., 64, 78
Ferguson, Miriam A., 78
Ferro, Joe, 118
Fisher, William S., 25
Flores, General Juan, 49, 51
Foitios, Eugene, 117
Ford, John S., 30, 32, 33, 37, 39
Former Texas Rangers Association,
    92
Friend, Llerana, 6
Frontier Battalion, 48, 53–56

Fuentes, Albert, 94, 95, 110–113,
    115, 119, 122, 124
Funston, Major General Frederick,
    64

G

García, Martin, 98, 100, 110, 111,
    113, 116, 122, 123
Garner, John Nance, 13, 63
Garrison, Homer, 82, 83, 117, 153
Garza, Marcelo, 58
Glover, Sheriff Robert M., 59
Goldstein, Kenneth, 40
González, Father Anthony, 133
González, Jesús, 60, 61
Goodwyn, Larry, 108, 109, 112
Guadalupe-Hidalgo, Treaty of, 31
Guerra, Joseph, 141
Gutiérrez, José Angel, 102, 125,
    127

H

Hale, A. J., 118
Hamer, Captain Frank, 78, 83
Hamm, Captain S. O., 82
Hays, Captain Jack, 25, 28, 30
Hays, John Coffee, 24, 26
Headquarters Division. *See* Texas
    Department of Public Safety.
Henderson, J. Pinckney, 27
Hernández, Mario, 101, 104, 115,
    118, 119
Herrera, Prudencio, 55
Hill, Attorney General John L.,
    163
Holmsback, Major B. H., 98
Homer Garrison Memorial Texas
    Ranger Museum, 7
Houston, Sam, 21, 22, 25, 26, 38
Humphreys, Parry W., 30
Huston, General Felix, 24

I

Independent Workers Association (IWA), 132
Ingraham, Joseph Holt, 39

J

Johnson, Lyndon Baines, 5, 147, 166
Jones, Major John B., 47, 53, 54
Juárez, Benito, 108

K

Karnes, Henry W., 23
Katz, Harvey, 9
Kenedy, Mifflin, 11, 51
Kennedy, John F., 94
Kennedy, Robert F., 116, 135
Killian, Father William, 139
Kindrick, Sam, 116
King Ranch, 57, 161
King, Richard, 11, 50
Kinney, H. L., 26
Krueger, Reverend Ed, 144, 146, 147, 150

L

La Casita Farms, 138, 148, 154, 155
La Raza Unida, 102, 127, 129, 137, 154
Lair, John B., 126
Lamar, Mirabeau B., 22, 23, 25, 26
Lara, Severita, 126, 128, 130
Las Cuevas Affair, 48
Lasswell, Mary, 4
Laughlin, Judge C. W., 154
Lee, Robert E., 37
ley de fuga, 54, 55
"Little Underground Railroad," 11

Lomax, John A., 40
Lopez, Abel, Jr., 94
Lopez, Brigido, 148, 149
"los tejanos sangrientos," 29
Lucey, Archbishop Robert E., 134
Lytle, James T., 40

M

McCulloch, Captain Ben, 24
McDonald, William, 6
McGee, Adjutant General Mark, 74
McNelly, Captain Leander H., 47–53
Maldonado, Manuel, 101, 114
Manifest Destiny, 11
Medrano v. *Allee*, 133, 136, 137, 139, 154, 156
Mendiola, Enrique, 51
Mendoza, Reynaldo, 101, 114, 119
Mexican American Joint Conference, 13
Mexican American Legal Defense Fund (MALDEF), 126
Mexican American Youth Organization (MAYO), 127
Mexican-American War, 2, 27
Mexican Revolution of 1910, 63
Minor, Judge R. B., 71, 73
Moore, Carlos, 95, 103, 105, 108
Moore, John H., 24
Moreno, Alex, 151
Morris, Sheriff W. T., 58, 59
"Mounted Riflemen", 21
"mounted volunteers", 22, 23
Muñoz, Henry, 95, 96, 99, 104, 106, 107, 109, 112, 114, 135

N

National Farm Workers Association (NFWA), 132

National Labor Relations Board, 140

Neff, Governor Pat, 68, 69, 71

Nelson, Eugene, 132, 134, 139, 140, 141

Nesbitt, Carl, 80

Nixon, Richard M., 5, 166

Novarro, Reverend James L., 133

Nye, Randall, 141, 142

O

O'Daniel, Governor W. Lee, 84

Oswandel, J. J., 28

P

Padilla, Gilbert, 138, 139

Paredes, Américo, 13, 39, 41, 42, 44, 55, 57, 60

Pecos River, 16

Peña, Albert A., Jr., 94, 95, 98, 141

Peoples, Captain Clint, 85

Permanent Council, 18

Phares, L. G., 80, 82

Plan de San Diego, 64

Political Association of Spanish Speaking Organizations (PASO), 94, 97, 103, 121, 122, 124

R

Ranger Hall of Fame, 7

"ranging companies," 22

"ranging men," 77

Reuther, Roy, 147

reverse racism, 111

"Rinches," 7, 149

Rio Grande River, 16, 17, 25

Rio Grande City, Texas, 131

Rodríguez, Benito, 151

Rodríguez, Tomás M., 117

Roebuck, W. E., 57

Rogers, Captain J. H., 60, 61

Royal Canadian Mounted Police, 1

Rubí, Marquis de, 16

S

San Francisco de los Patos, Mexico, 29

Sánchez, George E., 13, 141

Sánchez Navarro, Don Jacobo, 29

Scott, General Winfield, 28

Serna, Diana, 128

Shafer, Ray, 113, 119, 121

Shears, Robert, 34

Somerville, General Alexander, 25

Spears, Adrian, 116

Spears, J. L., 129

Special Rangers, 79, 80, 161, 163, 164, 166

Speir, Colonel Wilson E., 40

Sterling, Governor Ross, 78

Stilwell, Hart, 121, 122

Sweeten, Sheriff C. L., 105, 115, 119, 130

T

Taylor, Jay, 105

Taylor, General Zachary, 27, 28

Texans for the Educational Advancement of Mexican Americans (TEAM), 128

Texas, history of, colonization, 17, 18 independence, 18 statehood, 2, 26, 31

Texas Advisory Committee, 142

Texas Council of Churches, 146, 147

Texas Department of Public Safety, 77, 79, 80–85

Texas Highway Patrol, 79, 80, 81

Texas Observer, 108, 112, 113, 114, 116, 121, 140, 149, 150
Texas Public Health Service, 81
Texas Rangers, The, 5
Texas Rangers
  as cowboy, 3
  as paramilitary force, 15
  as symbol, 8
  as "troublemakers," 28
  creation of "rangers," 17, 18, 19, 21–23
  function of, 10, 11, 15, 56, 81, 84, 161
  image of, 2–7, 39–45
  investigation of, 12, 13, 66, 67
  official recognition of, 26
  qualifications for, 159–160
  role of, 1, 2
Texas Revolution, 2, 18, 19, 21
Tobin, Sheriff John, 68
Tobin, Captain W. G., 35, 36
Treaty of Guadalupe-Hidalgo, 31
Trevino, Armando, 126, 128
Trophy Farms, 138

U

United Farm Workers Organizing Committee, 138–140, 142–143
United States Army, 31
United States Cavalry, 10

United States Commission on Civil Rights, 10, 142
United States Supreme Court, 131, 155, 156

V

Van Cleave, Sergeant Jack, 96, 146
Vasquez, Rafael, 25
Veteran's Bar, 106
Villa, Pancho, 64

W

Weaver, John, 6
Webb, Walter Prescott, 5–7, 11, 19–21, 27–30, 39, 51–53, 56, 67, 68, 83, 166
Westerman, Max, 84
Williamson, R. M., 19
Wilson, Captain Bill, 86, 160, 161
Wilson, R. B., 161, 162
Wilson, Woodrow, 64, 65
Wood, George T., 28

Y

Yarborough, Senator Ralph, 13, 116, 118, 123, 128, 134, 135, 149, 159

Z

Zimmerman Note, 64